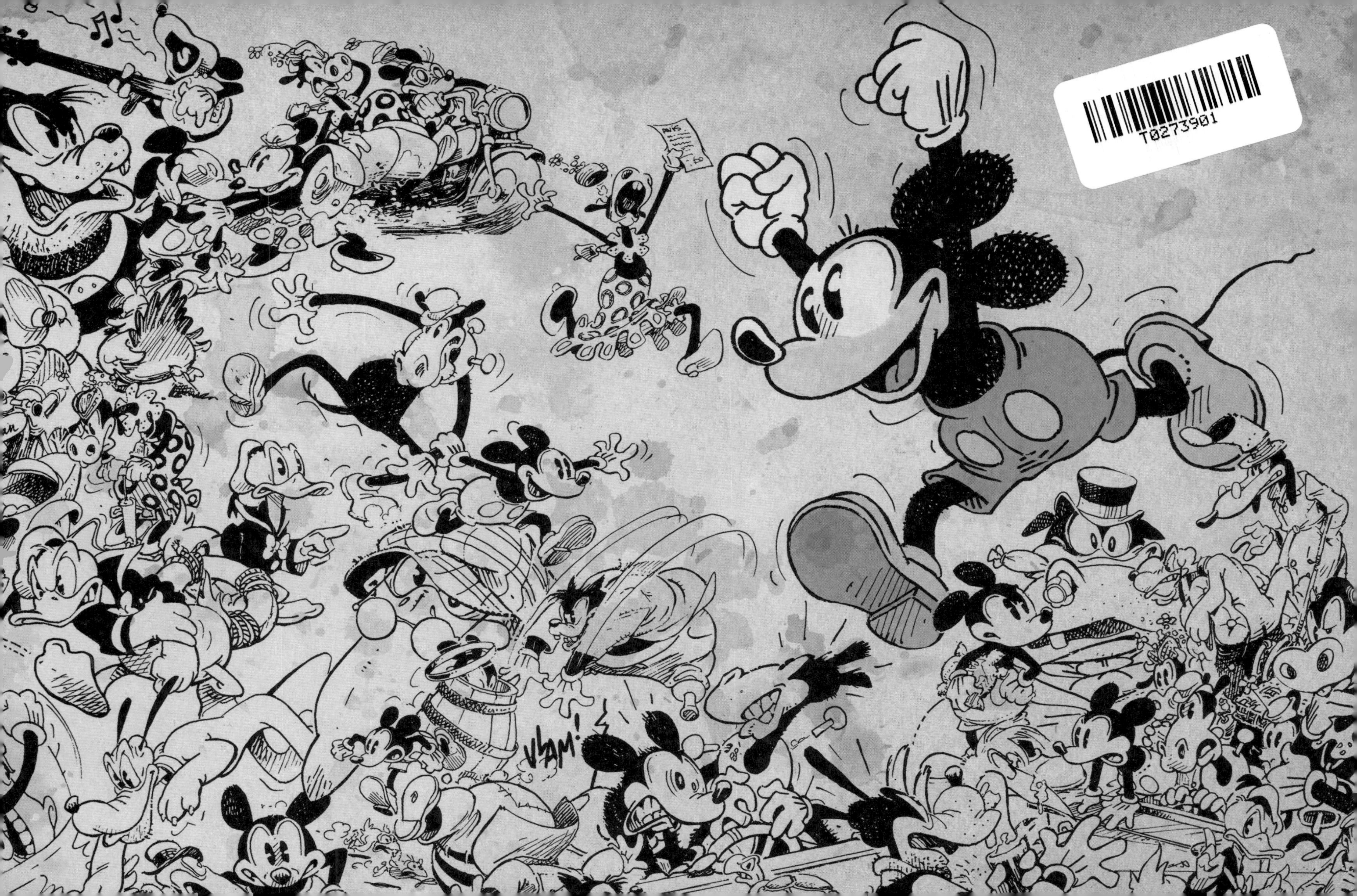
AVIS
VLAM!

Publisher: GARY GROTH
Editor: DAVID GERSTEIN
Translation and Dialogue: DAVID GERSTEIN
Designer: JUSTIN ALLAN-SPENCER
Lettering and Production: PAUL BARESH and CHRISTINA HWANG
Associate Publisher: ERIC REYNOLDS

Fantagraphics Books, Inc.
7563 Lake City Way NE
Seattle WA 98115
(800) 657-1100

Visit us at fantagraphics.com
Follow us on Twitter at @fantagraphics
and on Facebook at facebook.com/fantagraphics.

First printing: May 2022
ISBN 978-1-68396-437-7
eBook ISBN 978-1-68396-592-3
Printed in China
Library of Congress Control Number: 2020950115

The feature story in this volume was first published in France, and
appears here in English for the first time.

ALSO AVAILABLE

Mickey All-Stars
40 international artists, including Giorgio Cavazzano and Mike Peraza

Walt Disney's Uncle Scrooge: The Golden Nugget Boat
Carl Barks

Mickey Mouse: Trapped in the Shadow Dimension
Andrea "Casty" Castellan; *Disney Masters* Vol. 19

Donald Duck: 20,000 Leaks Under the Sea
Dick Kinney and Al Hubbard; *Disney Masters* Vol. 20

The Complete Life and Times of Scrooge McDuck Deluxe Edition
Don Rosa

FROM OUR NON-DISNEY CATALOG

Nuft and the Last Dragons: By Balloon to the North Pole
Freddy Milton

Walt Disney

MICKEY MOUSE

Zombie Coffee

STORY, ART AND COLOR BY

Régis Loisel

COVER COLOR BY FRANCOIS LAPIERRE

I dedicate this book to many writers and artists.

Starting, of course, with Walt Disney and his partner Ub Iwerks, the genius who visually designed Mickey Mouse and knew how to bring him to life.

And then the others: all of those who have contributed to the development of the fabulous Mouseton and Duckburg universe:

Floyd Gottfredson (and his inkers Ted Thwaites and Bill Wright), Al Taliaferro, Manuel Gonzales, Carl Barks, Paul Murry...

Not to forget Pat Sullivan and Otto Messmer (*Felix the Cat*), George Herriman (*Krazy Kat*), Rudolph Dirks and Harold Knerr (*The Katzenjammer Kids*), Billy DeBeck (*Barney Google and Snuffy Smith*), Cliff Sterrett (*Polly and Her Pals*), George McManus (*Bringing Up Father*), James F. Davis (*The Fox and the Crow*), Elzie Segar (*Popeye*), Tex Avery (*Looney Tunes, Droopy*)...

And of course, physically closer to me here in Europe, there are Jean Cézard (*Arthur le fantome justicier*), Morris (*Lucky Luke*), André Franquin (*Spirou, Gomer Goof*), Marten Toonder (*Tom Puss*), Romano Scarpa and Giorgio Cavazzano, and of course our great Albert Uderzo (*Asterix*).

I also have an especial fondness for all the ghost artists whose names we don't know...

Apologies if I've forgotten some of those who came before me. There are so many of them.

Together, they form a long creative chain to which I've been lucky enough to add a link.

And one day, Jacques Glénat — founder of the French printing house that first published "Zombie Coffee" — remembered that creating a Mickey Mouse story was one of my longtime dreams...

Thank you for that!

Many thanks also to **François Lapierre**, for contributing to the digital enhancement of my color.

Régis Loisel

This content has been reprinted in its entirety as first created in 2016.

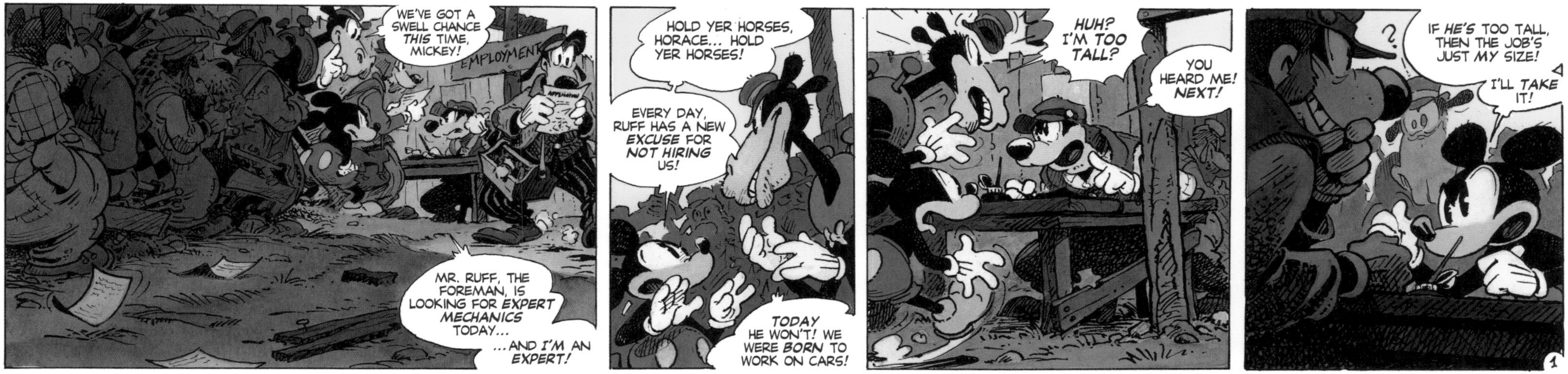
WE'VE GOT A SWELL CHANCE THIS TIME, MICKEY!
EMPLOYMENT
APPLICATION
MR. RUFF, THE FOREMAN, IS LOOKING FOR EXPERT MECHANICS TODAY...
...AND I'M AN EXPERT!
HOLD YER HORSES, HORACE... HOLD YER HORSES!
EVERY DAY, RUFF HAS A NEW EXCUSE FOR NOT HIRING US!
TODAY HE WON'T! WE WERE BORN TO WORK ON CARS!
HUH? I'M TOO TALL?
YOU HEARD ME! NEXT!
?
IF HE'S TOO TALL, THEN THE JOB'S JUST MY SIZE!
I'LL TAKE IT!
1

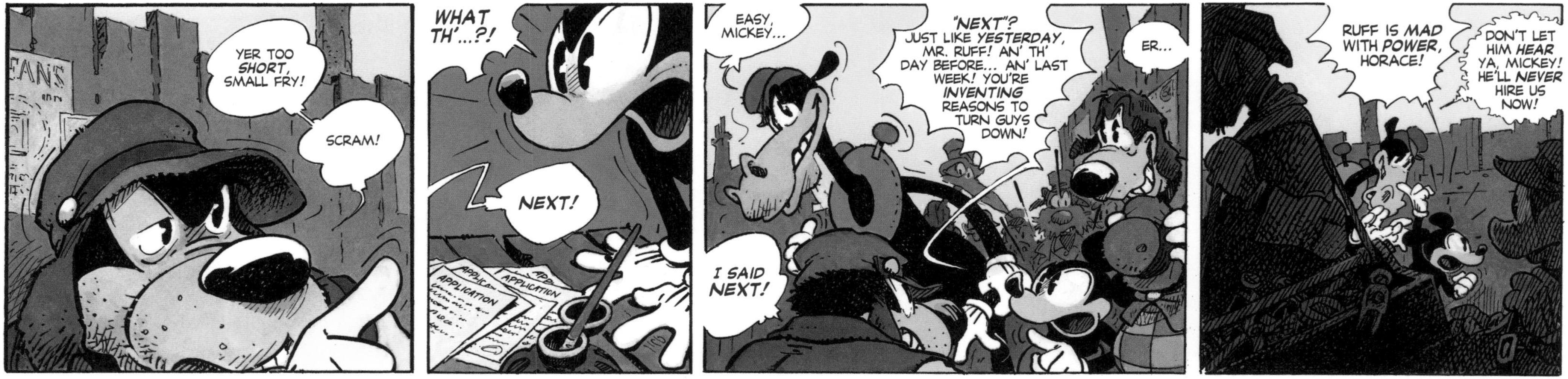
YER TOO SHORT, SMALL FRY!
SCRAM!
WHAT TH'...?!
NEXT!
APPLICATION
APPLICATION
EASY, MICKEY...
"NEXT"? JUST LIKE YESTERDAY, MR. RUFF! AN' TH' DAY BEFORE... AN' LAST WEEK! YOU'RE INVENTING REASONS TO TURN GUYS DOWN!
ER...
I SAID NEXT!
RUFF IS MAD WITH POWER, HORACE!
DON'T LET HIM HEAR YA, MICKEY! HE'LL NEVER HIRE US NOW!

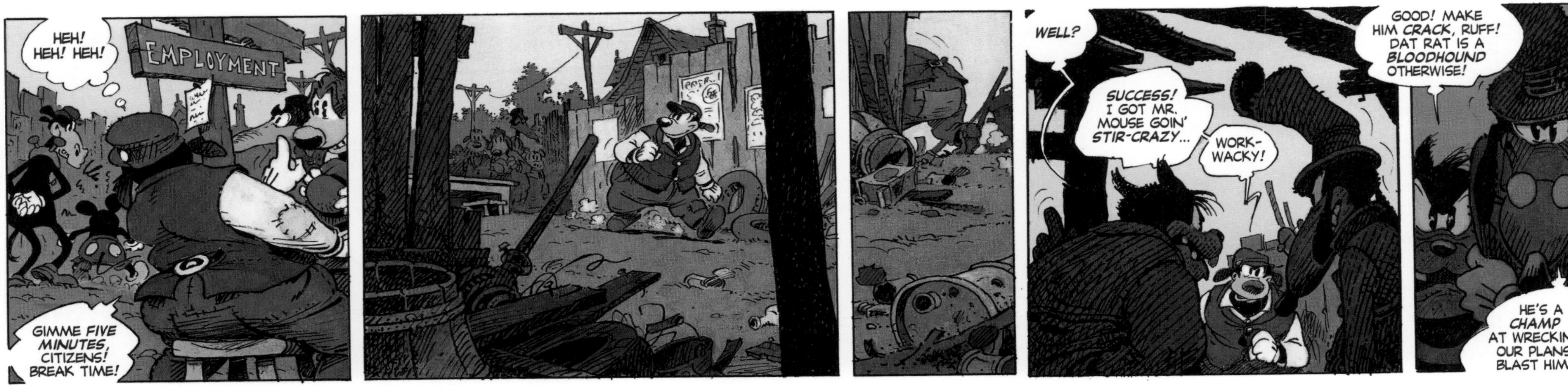
HEH! HEH! HEH!
EMPLOYMENT
GIMME FIVE MINUTES, CITIZENS! BREAK TIME!
WELL?
SUCCESS! I GOT MR. MOUSE GOIN' STIR-CRAZY...
WORK-WACKY!
GOOD! MAKE HIM CRACK, RUFF! DAT RAT IS A BLOODHOUND OTHERWISE!
HE'S A CHAMP AT WRECKING OUR PLANS, BLAST HIM!

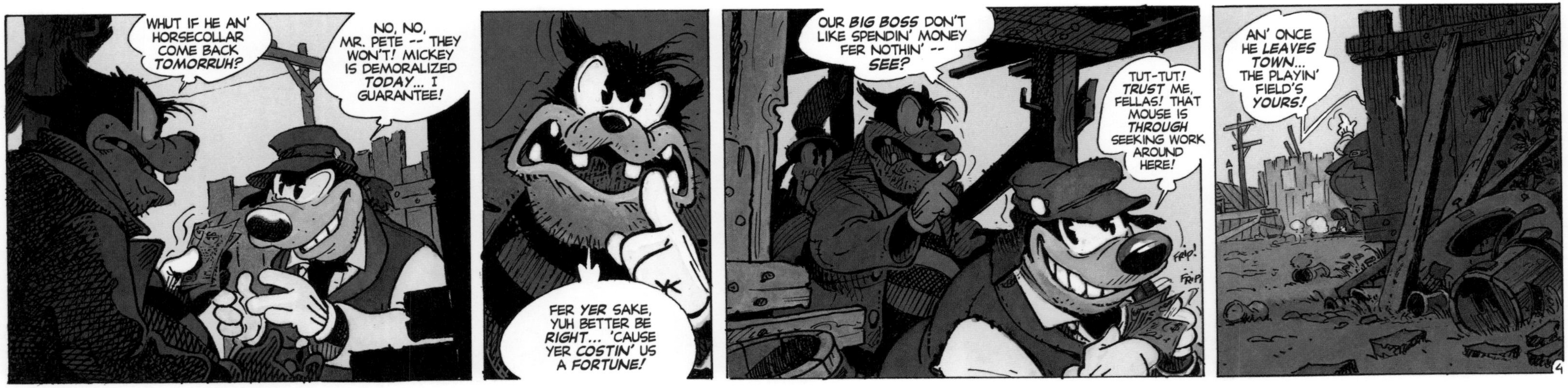
WHUT IF HE AN' HORSECOLLAR COME BACK TOMORRUH?
NO, NO, MR. PETE -- THEY WON'T! MICKEY IS DEMORALIZED TODAY... I GUARANTEE!
FER YER SAKE, YUH BETTER BE RIGHT... 'CAUSE YER COSTIN' US A FORTUNE!
OUR BIG BOSS DON'T LIKE SPENDIN' MONEY FER NOTHIN' -- SEE?
TUT-TUT! TRUST ME, FELLAS! THAT MOUSE IS THROUGH SEEKING WORK AROUND HERE!
AN' ONCE HE LEAVES TOWN... THE PLAYIN' FIELD'S YOURS!

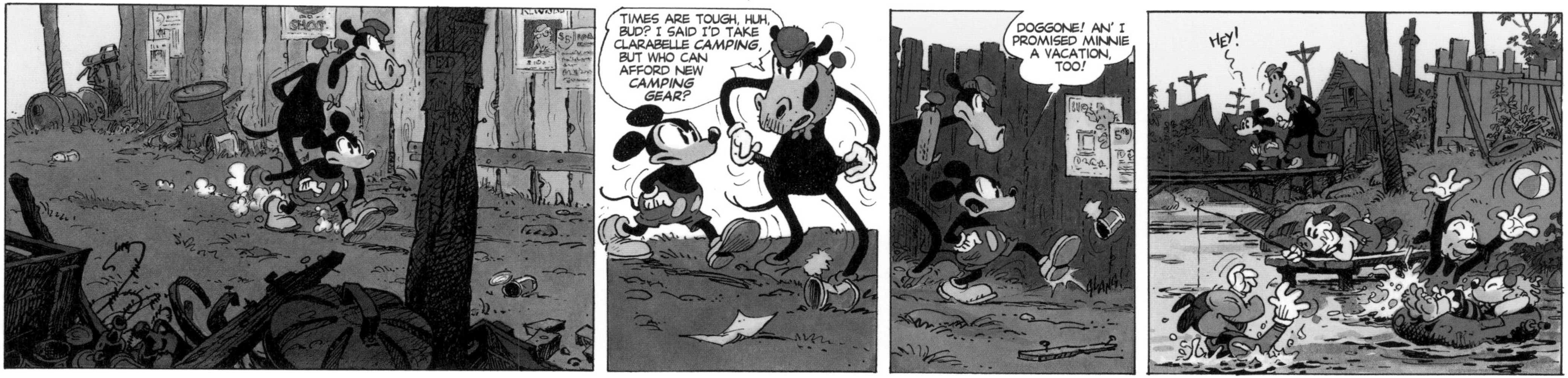
TIMES ARE TOUGH, HUH, BUD? I SAID I'D TAKE CLARABELLE CAMPING, BUT WHO CAN AFFORD NEW CAMPING GEAR?
DOGGONE! AN' I PROMISED MINNIE A VACATION, TOO!
HEY!

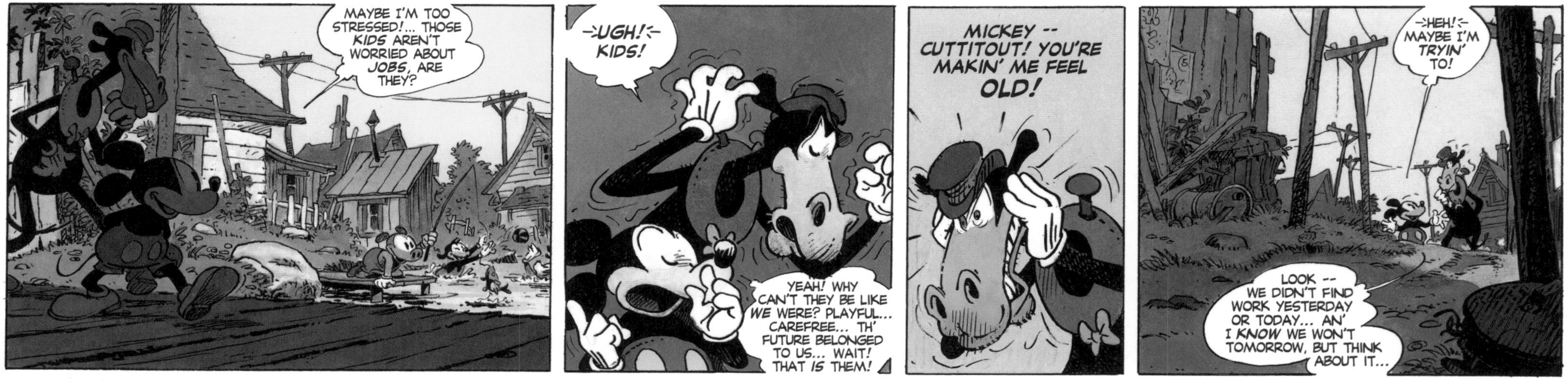
MAYBE I'M TOO STRESSED!... THOSE KIDS AREN'T WORRIED ABOUT JOBS, ARE THEY?
UGH! KIDS!
YEAH! WHY CAN'T THEY BE LIKE WE WERE? PLAYFUL... CAREFREE... TH' FUTURE BELONGED TO US... WAIT! THAT IS THEM!
MICKEY -- CUTTITOUT! YOU'RE MAKIN' ME FEEL OLD!
HEH! MAYBE I'M TRYIN' TO!
LOOK -- WE DIDN'T FIND WORK YESTERDAY OR TODAY... AN' I KNOW WE WON'T TOMORROW, BUT THINK ABOUT IT...

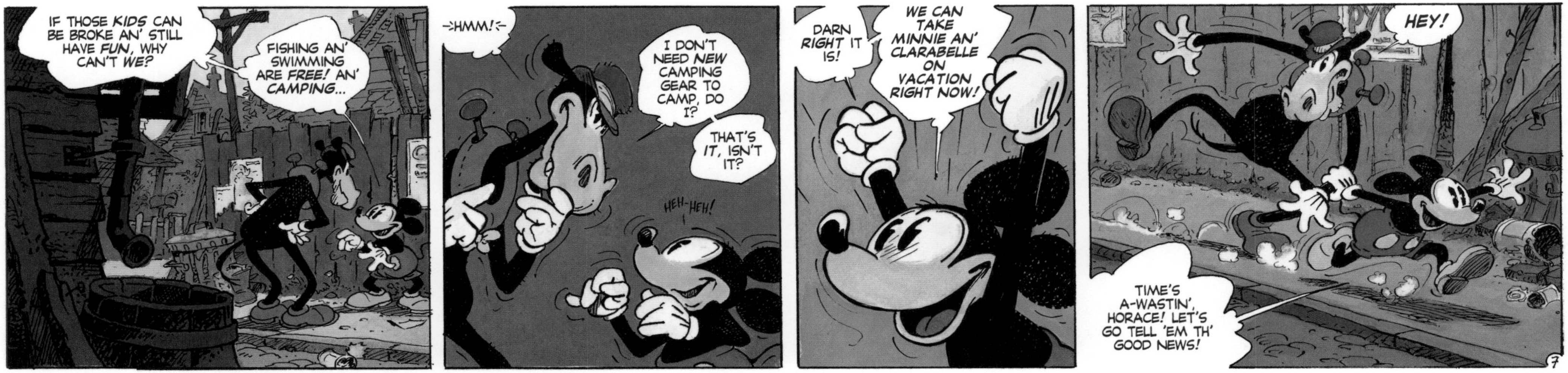
IF THOSE *KIDS* CAN BE BROKE AN' STILL HAVE *FUN*, WHY CAN'T *WE*?
FISHING AN' SWIMMING ARE *FREE!* AN' *CAMPING*...
–>HMM!<–
I DON'T NEED *NEW* CAMPING GEAR TO CAMP, DO I?
THAT'S *IT*, ISN'T IT?
HEH-HEH!
DARN *RIGHT* IT IS!
WE CAN TAKE MINNIE AN' CLARABELLE ON VACATION RIGHT NOW!
HEY!
TIME'S A-WASTIN', HORACE*!* LET'S GO TELL 'EM TH' GOOD NEWS*!*
7

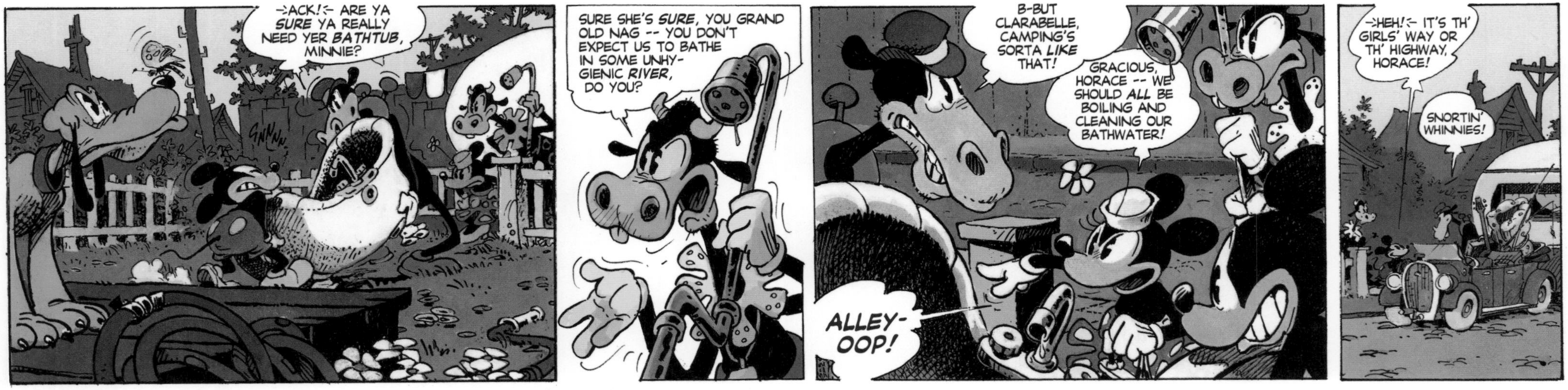
–>ACK!<– ARE YA *SURE* YA REALLY NEED YER *BATHTUB*, MINNIE?
SURE SHE'S *SURE*, YOU GRAND OLD NAG -- YOU DON'T EXPECT US TO BATHE IN SOME UNHY-GIENIC *RIVER*, DO YOU?
B-BUT CLARABELLE, CAMPING'S SORTA *LIKE* THAT!
GRACIOUS, HORACE -- WE SHOULD *ALL* BE BOILING AND CLEANING OUR BATHWATER!
ALLEY-OOP!
–>HEH!<– IT'S TH' GIRLS' WAY OR TH' HIGHWAY, HORACE!
SNORTIN' WHINNIES!

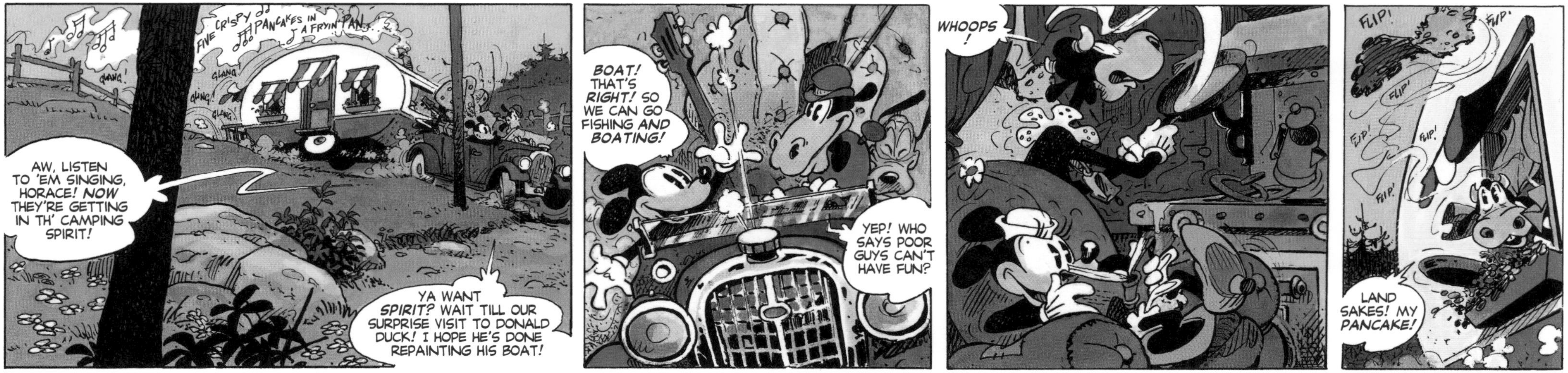
GLANG!
FIVE CRISPY PANCAKES IN A FRYIN' PAN...
GLANG!
GLING!
GLANG!
AW, LISTEN TO 'EM SINGING, HORACE! NOW THEY'RE GETTING IN TH' CAMPING SPIRIT!
YA WANT SPIRIT? WAIT TILL OUR SURPRISE VISIT TO DONALD DUCK! I HOPE HE'S DONE REPAINTING HIS BOAT!
BOAT! THAT'S RIGHT! SO WE CAN GO FISHING AND BOATING!
YEP! WHO SAYS POOR GUYS CAN'T HAVE FUN?
WHOOPS!
FLIP!
FLIP!
FLIP!
FLIP!
FLIP!
FLIP!
LAND SAKES! MY PANCAKE!

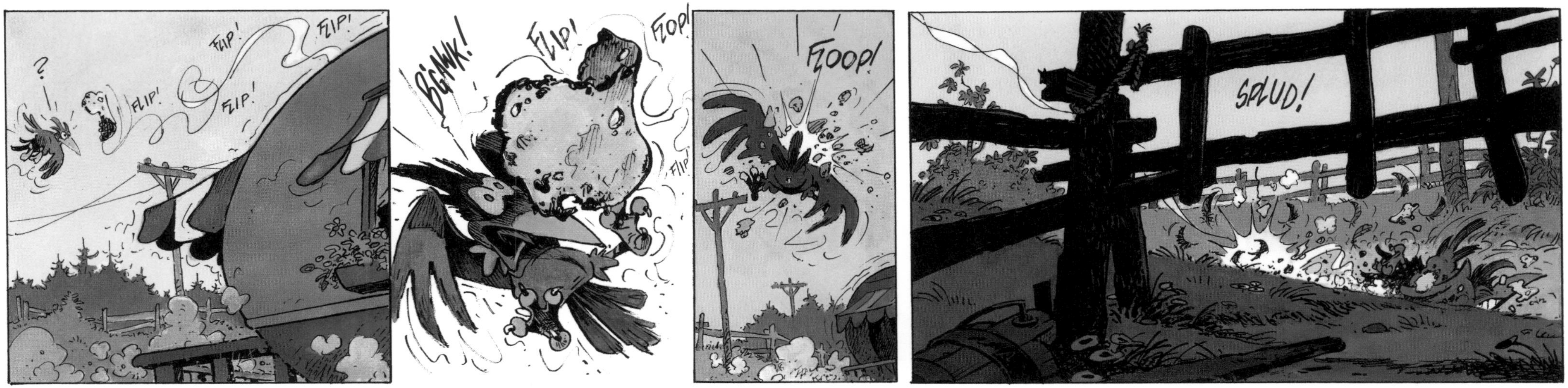
?
FLIP!
FLIP!
FLIP!
FLIP!
BGAWK!
FLIP!
FLOP!
FLIP!
FLOOP!
SPLUD!

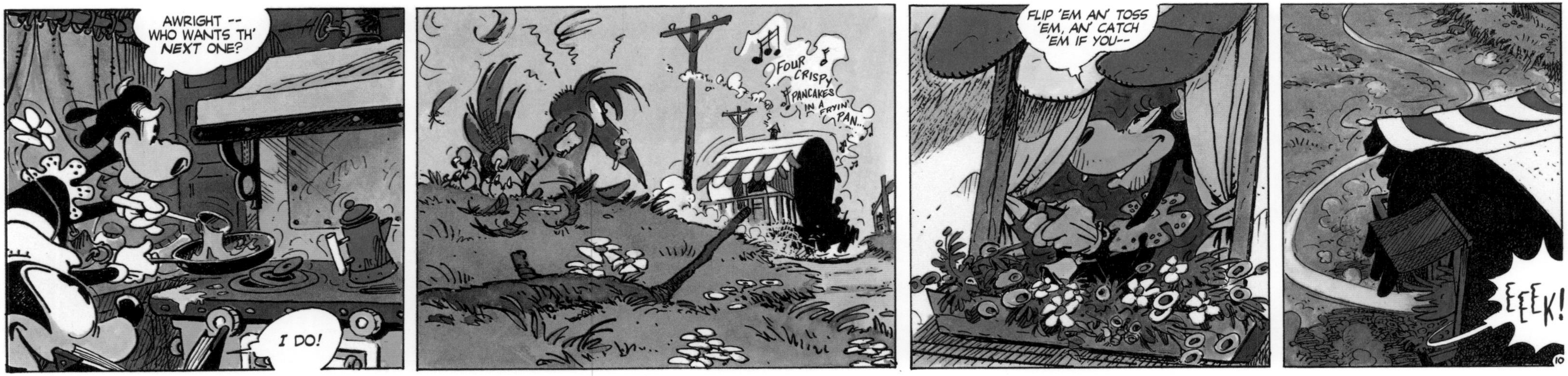
AWRIGHT -- WHO WANTS TH' NEXT ONE?
I DO!
FOUR CRISPY PANCAKES IN A FRYIN' PAN...
FLIP 'EM AN' TOSS 'EM, AN' CATCH 'EM IF YOU--
EEEK!
10

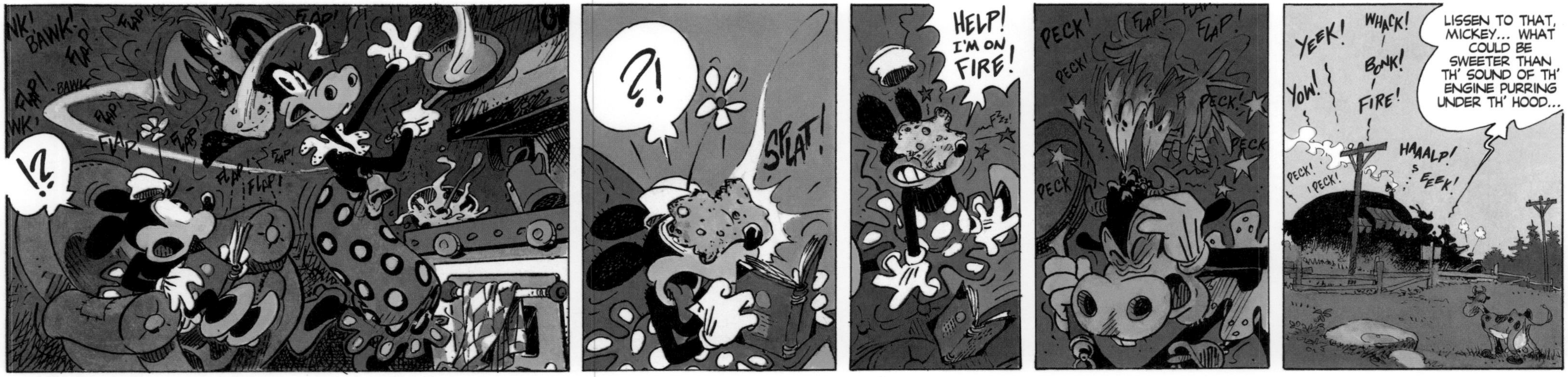
BAWK!
FLAP!
!?
?!
SPLAT!
HELP! I'M ON FIRE!
PECK!
PECK!
FLAP!
PECK!
YEEK!
WHACK!
YOW!
BONK!
FIRE!
PECK!
PECK!
HAAALP!
EEEK!
LISSEN TO THAT, MICKEY... WHAT COULD BE SWEETER THAN TH' SOUND OF TH' ENGINE PURRING UNDER TH' HOOD...

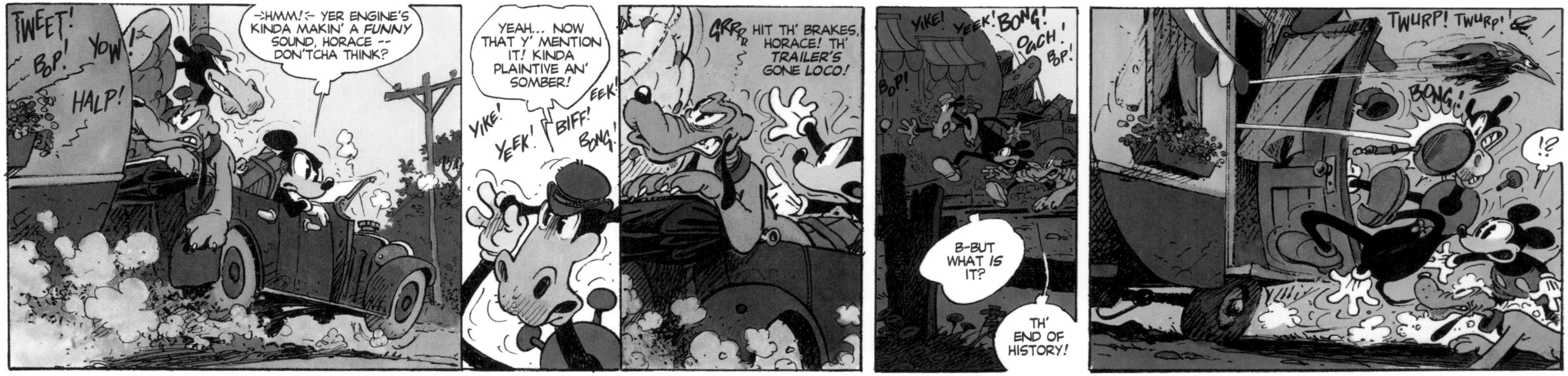
TWEET!
BOP!
YOW!
HALP!
-HMM!- YER ENGINE'S KINDA MAKIN' A *FUNNY* SOUND, HORACE -- DON'TCHA THINK?
YEAH... NOW THAT Y' MENTION IT! KINDA PLAINTIVE AN' SOMBER!
YIKE!
YEEK!
BIFF!
EEK!
BONG!
GRRR
HIT TH' BRAKES, HORACE! TH' *TRAILER'S* GONE *LOCO!*
YIKE!
YEEK!
BONG!
OOCH!
BOP!
BOP!
B-BUT WHAT *IS* IT?
TH' END OF HISTORY!
TWURP! TWURP!
BONG!
!?

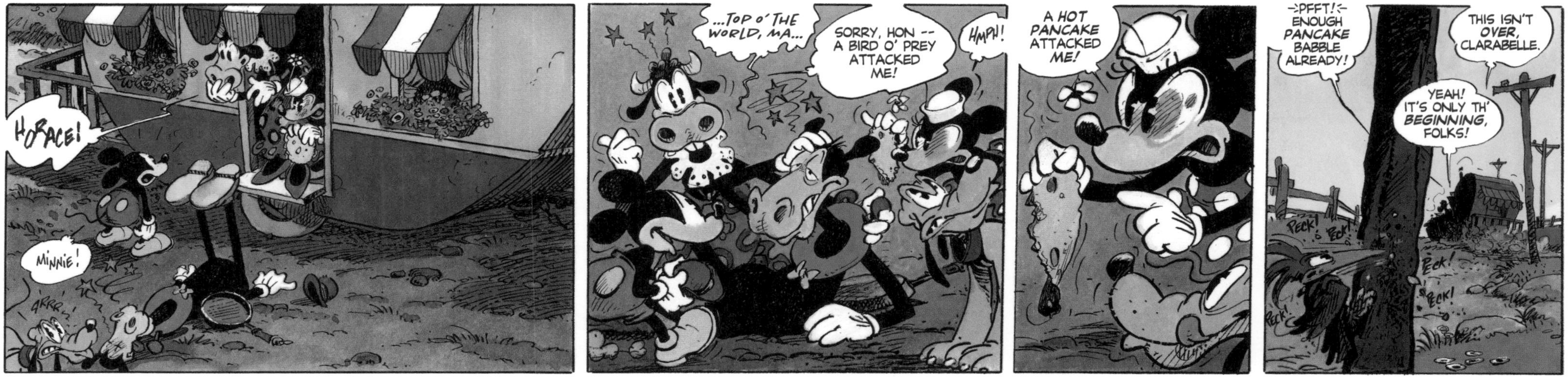
HORACE!
MINNIE!
...TOP O' THE WORLD, MA...
SORRY, HON -- A BIRD O' PREY ATTACKED ME!
HMPH!
A *HOT PANCAKE* ATTACKED *ME!*
-PFFT!- ENOUGH *PANCAKE* BABBLE ALREADY!
THIS ISN'T *OVER,* CLARABELLE.
YEAH! IT'S ONLY TH' *BEGINNING,* FOLKS!
PECK!
PECK!
PECK!
PECK!
PECK!

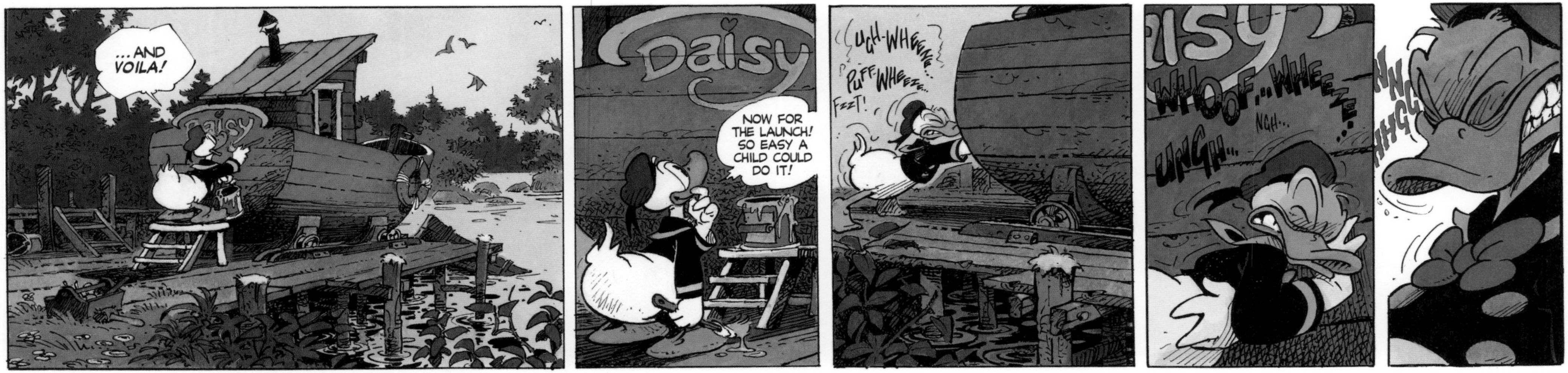
...AND VOILA!
NOW FOR THE LAUNCH! SO EASY A CHILD COULD DO IT!
UGH-WHEEZE...
PUFF-WHEEZE...
FZZT!
WHOOF...WHEEZE...
UNGH...
NGH...

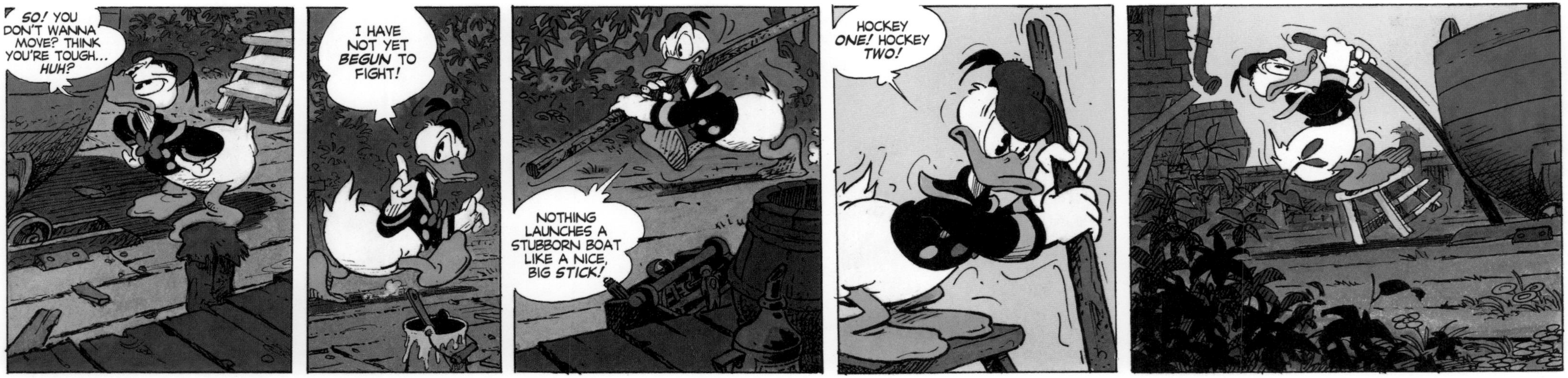
SO! YOU DON'T WANNA MOVE? THINK YOU'RE TOUGH... HUH?
I HAVE NOT YET BEGUN TO FIGHT!
NOTHING LAUNCHES A STUBBORN BOAT LIKE A NICE, BIG STICK!
HOCKEY ONE! HOCKEY TWO!

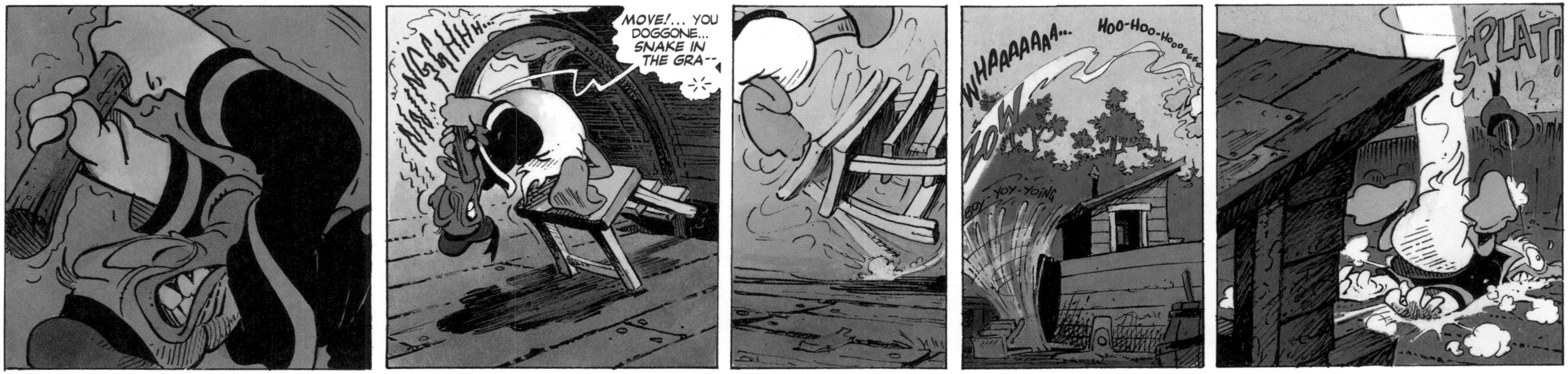
MOVE!... YOU DOGGONE... SNAKE IN THE GRA--
WHAAAAAA...
ZOW
BOY-YOY-YOING
SPLAT!

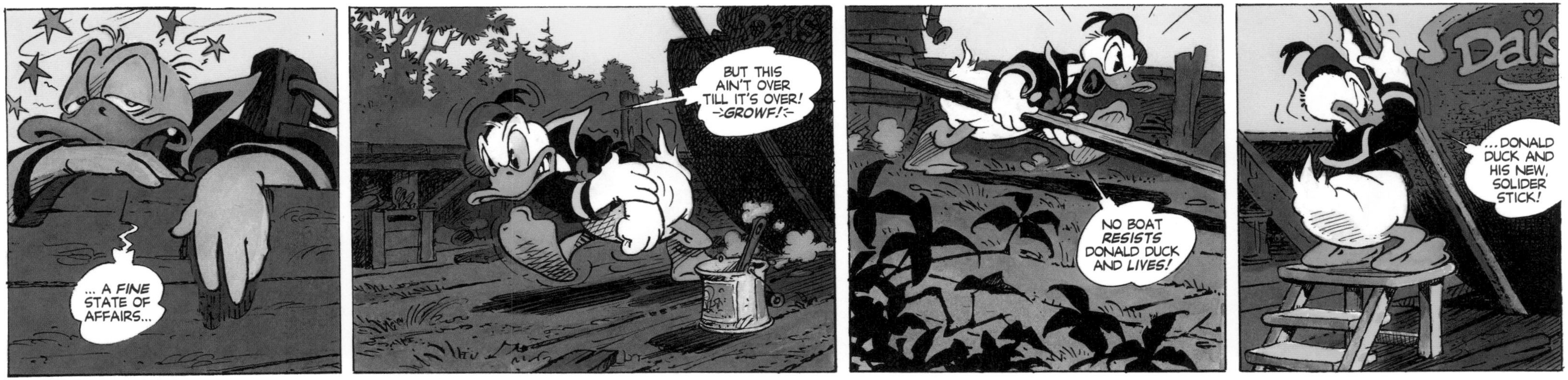
... A FINE STATE OF AFFAIRS...
BUT THIS AIN'T OVER TILL IT'S OVER! -GROWF!-
NO BOAT RESISTS DONALD DUCK AND LIVES!
...DONALD DUCK AND HIS NEW, SOLIDER STICK!

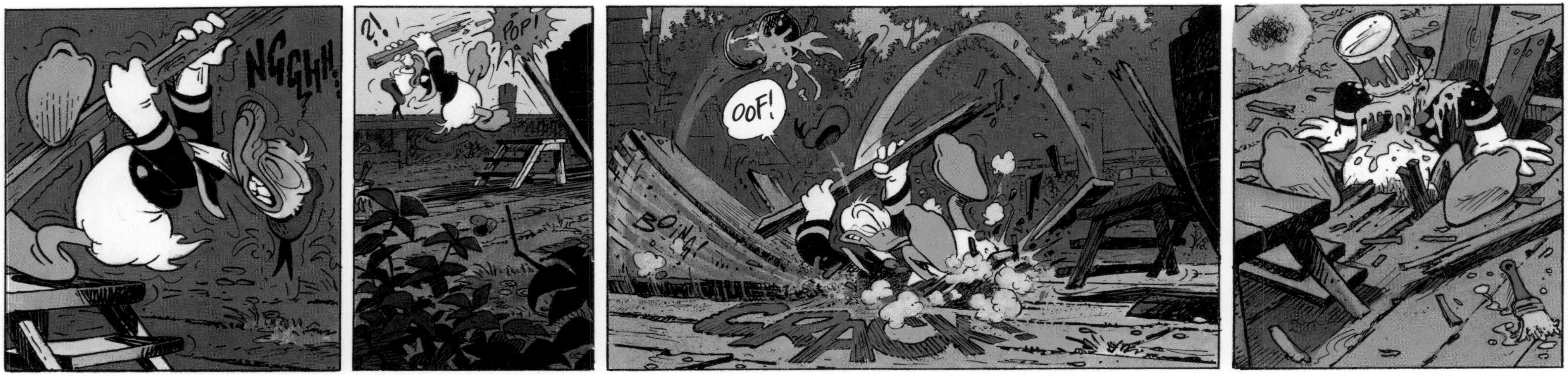
NGGHH!
?!
POP!
OOF!
BOING!
CRACK

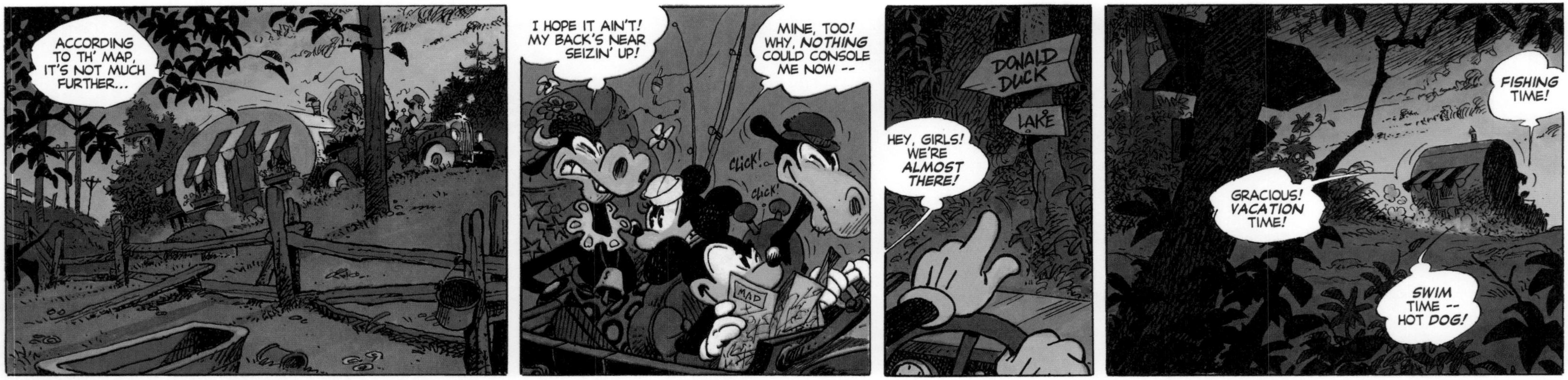
ACCORDING TO TH' MAP, IT'S NOT MUCH FURTHER...
I HOPE IT AIN'T! MY BACK'S NEAR SEIZIN' UP!
MINE, TOO! WHY, NOTHING COULD CONSOLE ME NOW --
CLICK!
CLICK!
DONALD DUCK
LAKE
HEY, GIRLS! WE'RE ALMOST THERE!
FISHING TIME!
GRACIOUS! VACATION TIME!
SWIM TIME -- HOT DOG!

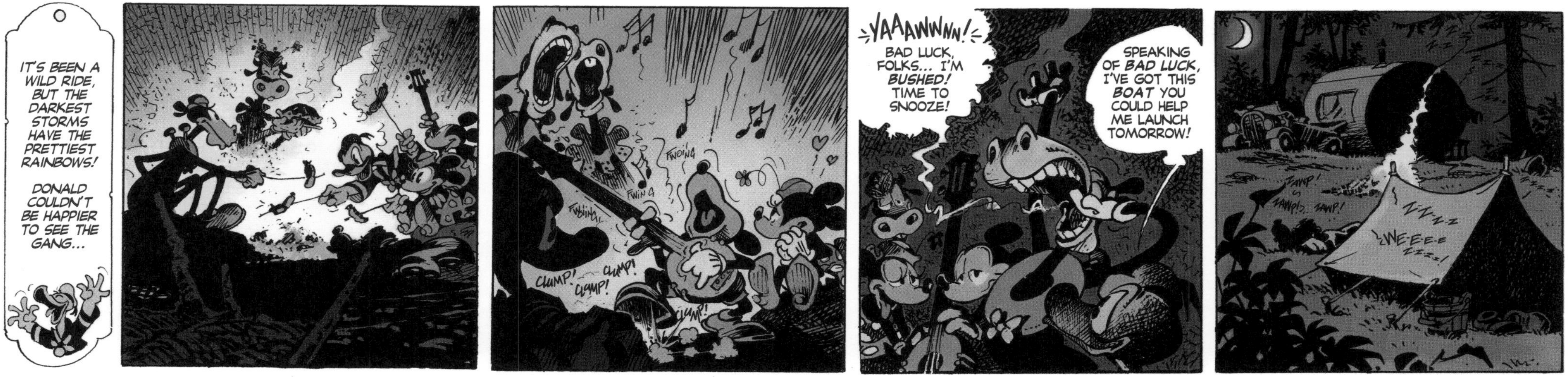
IT'S BEEN A WILD RIDE, BUT THE DARKEST STORMS HAVE THE PRETTIEST RAINBOWS!
DONALD COULDN'T BE HAPPIER TO SEE THE GANG...
FWOING
FWING
CLUMP!
CLUMP!
CLUMP!
CLUMP!
YAAAWWNN!
BAD LUCK, FOLKS... I'M BUSHED! TIME TO SNOOZE!
SPEAKING OF BAD LUCK, I'VE GOT THIS BOAT YOU COULD HELP ME LAUNCH TOMORROW!
Z-Z-Z-Z
WE-E-E-E Z-Z-Z-Z!

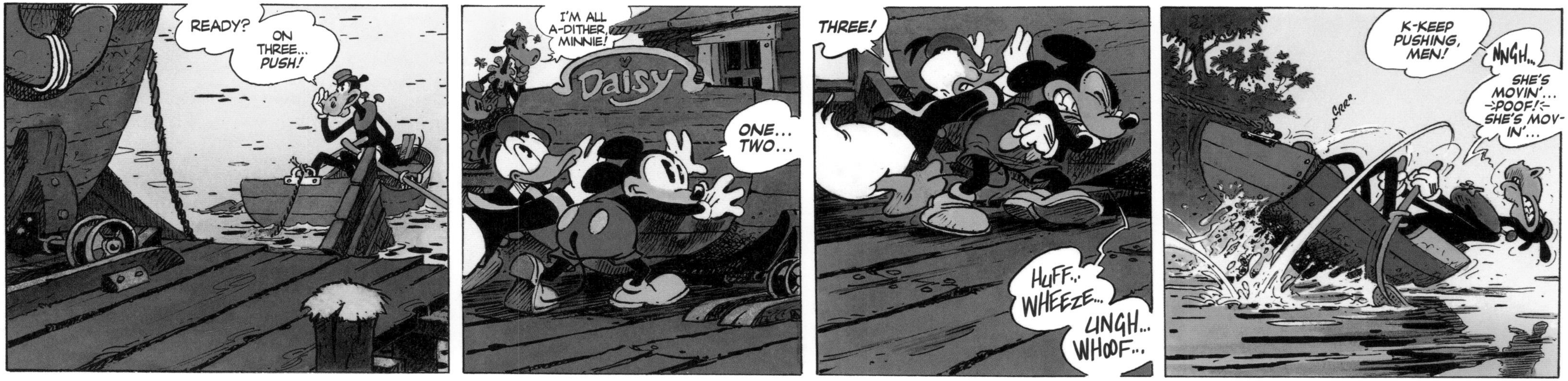
READY?
ON THREE... PUSH!
I'M ALL A-DITHER, MINNIE!
Daisy
ONE... TWO...
THREE!
HUFF.. WHEEZE...
UNGH... WHOOF...
K-KEEP PUSHING, MEN!
NNGH..
SHE'S MOVIN'... -POOF!- SHE'S MOV-IN'...

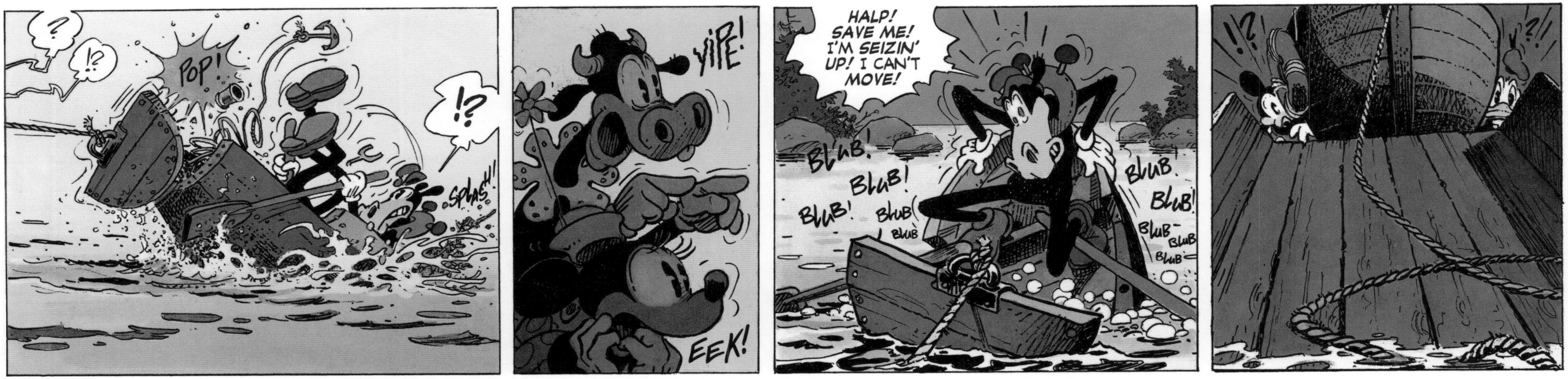
?
!?
POP!
!?
SPLASH!
YIPE!
EEK!
HALP! SAVE ME! I'M SEIZIN' UP! I CAN'T MOVE!
BLUB! BLUB! BLUB! BLUB! BLUB
BLUB BLUB! BLUB BLUB BLUB
!?
?!

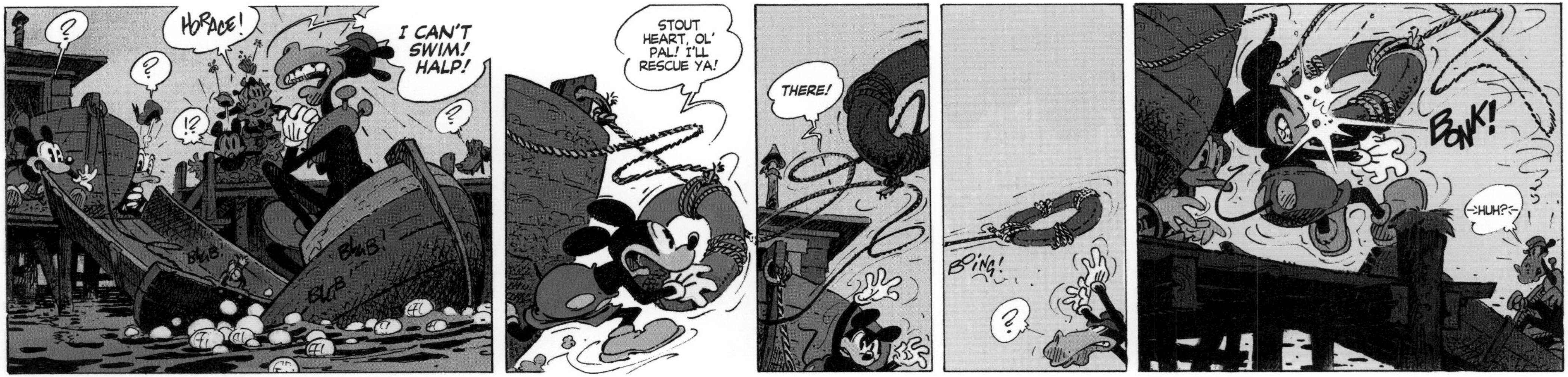
?
HORACE!
?
!?
I CAN'T SWIM! HALP!
?
BLUB!
BLUB!
BLUB
STOUT HEART, OL' PAL! I'LL RESCUE YA!
THERE!
BOING!
?
BONK!
HUH?

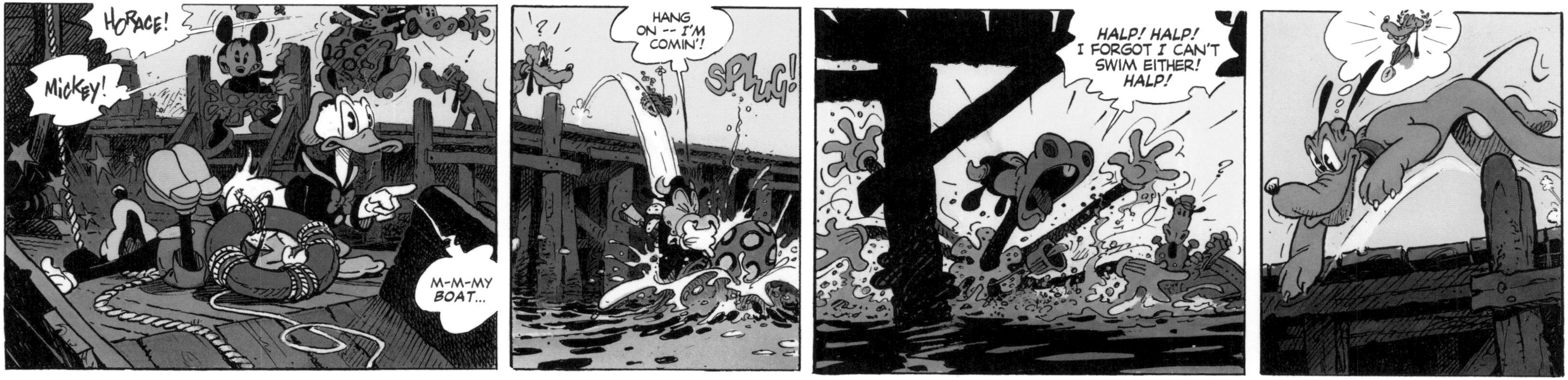
HORACE!
MICKEY!
M-M-MY BOAT...
HANG ON -- I'M COMIN'!
SPLUG!
HALP! HALP! I FORGOT I CAN'T SWIM EITHER! HALP!

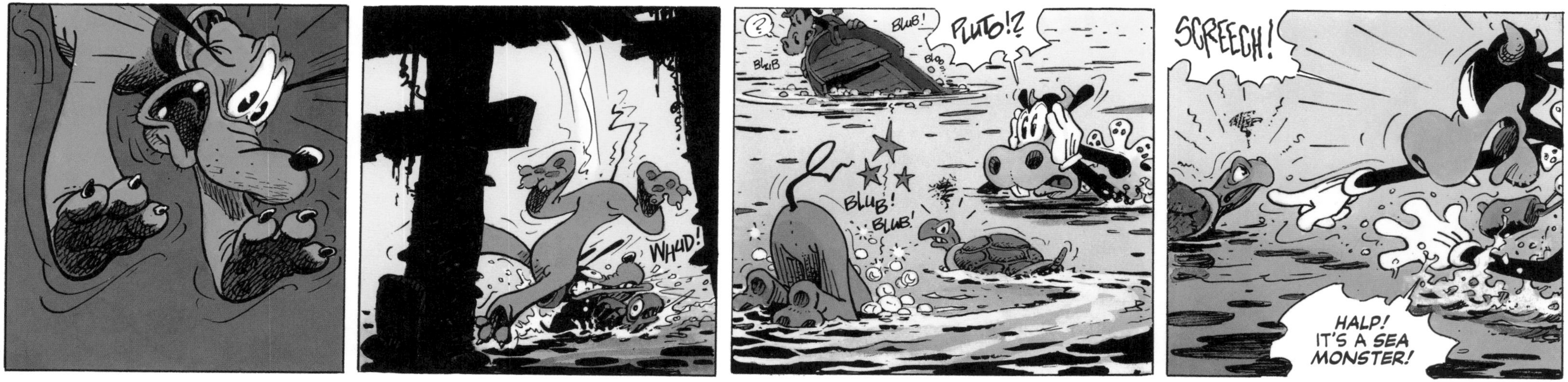
WHUD!
BLUB!
PLUTO!?
BLUB!
BLUB!
SCREECH!
HALP! IT'S A SEA MONSTER!

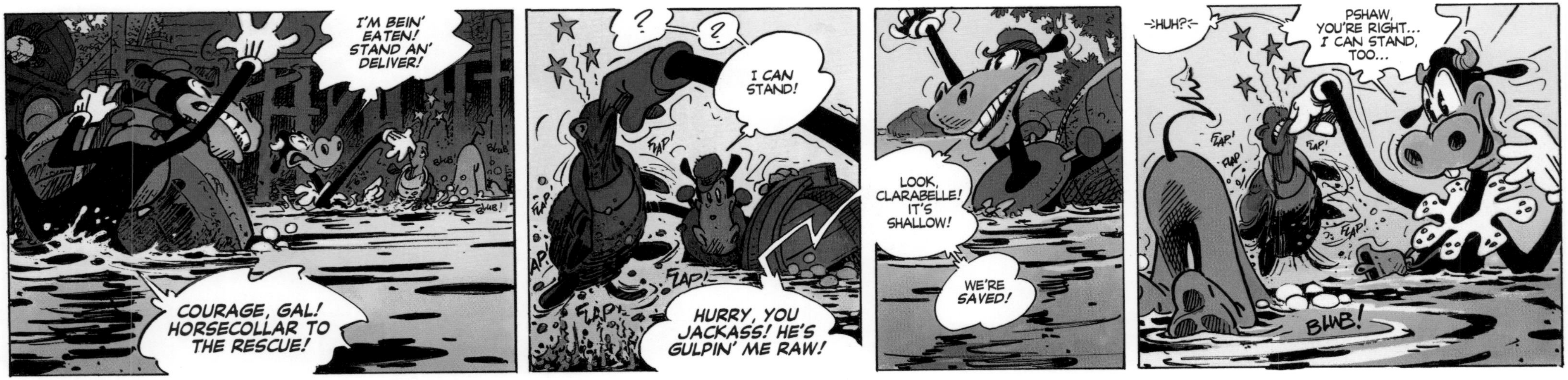
I'M BEIN' EATEN! STAND AN' DELIVER!
COURAGE, GAL! HORSECOLLAR TO THE RESCUE!
?
?
I CAN STAND!
FLAP!
HURRY, YOU JACKASS! HE'S GULPIN' ME RAW!
LOOK, CLARABELLE! IT'S SHALLOW!
WE'RE SAVED!
HUH?
PSHAW, YOU'RE RIGHT... I CAN STAND, TOO...
BLWB!

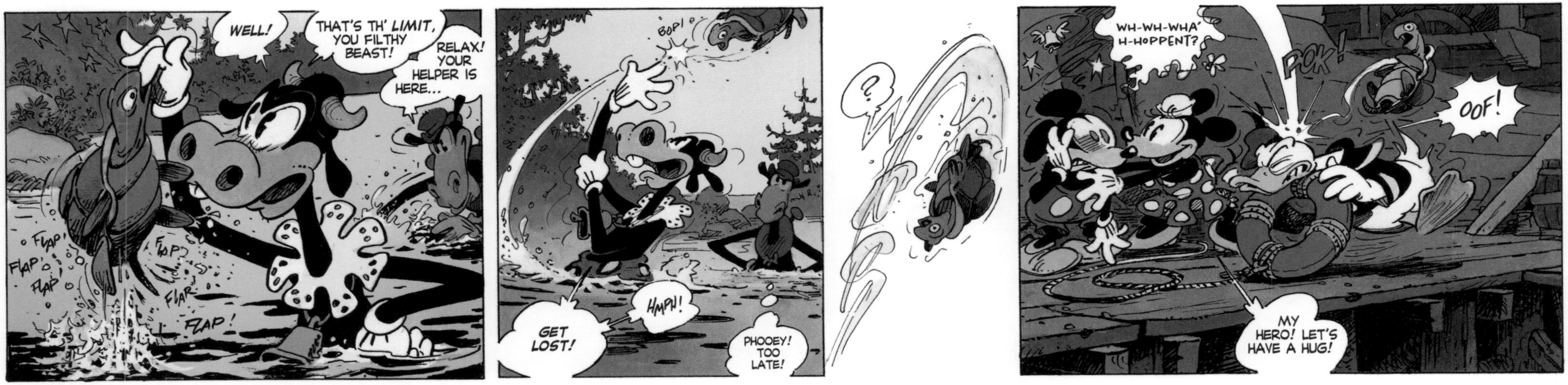
WELL!
THAT'S TH' LIMIT, YOU FILTHY BEAST!
RELAX! YOUR HELPER IS HERE...
FLAP!
BOP!
GET LOST!
HMPH!
PHOOEY! TOO LATE!
?
WH-WH-WHA' H-HOPPENT?
POK!
OOF!
MY HERO! LET'S HAVE A HUG!

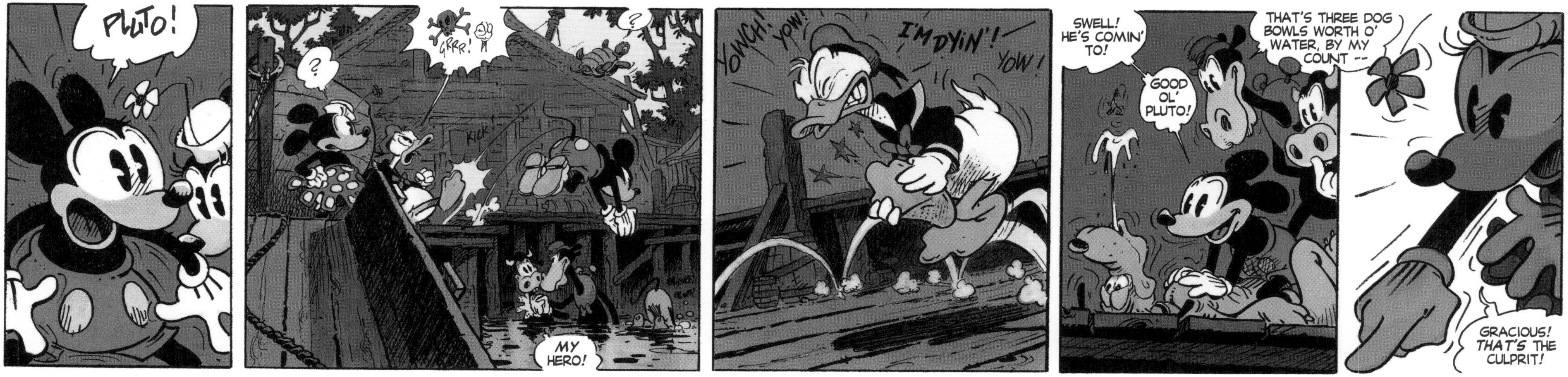
PLUTO!
?
GRRR!
?
KICK!
MY HERO!
YOWCH!
YOW!
I'M DYIN'!
YOW!
SWELL! HE'S COMIN' TO!
GOOD OL' PLUTO!
THAT'S THREE DOG BOWLS WORTH O' WATER, BY MY COUNT --
GRACIOUS! *THAT'S* THE CULPRIT!

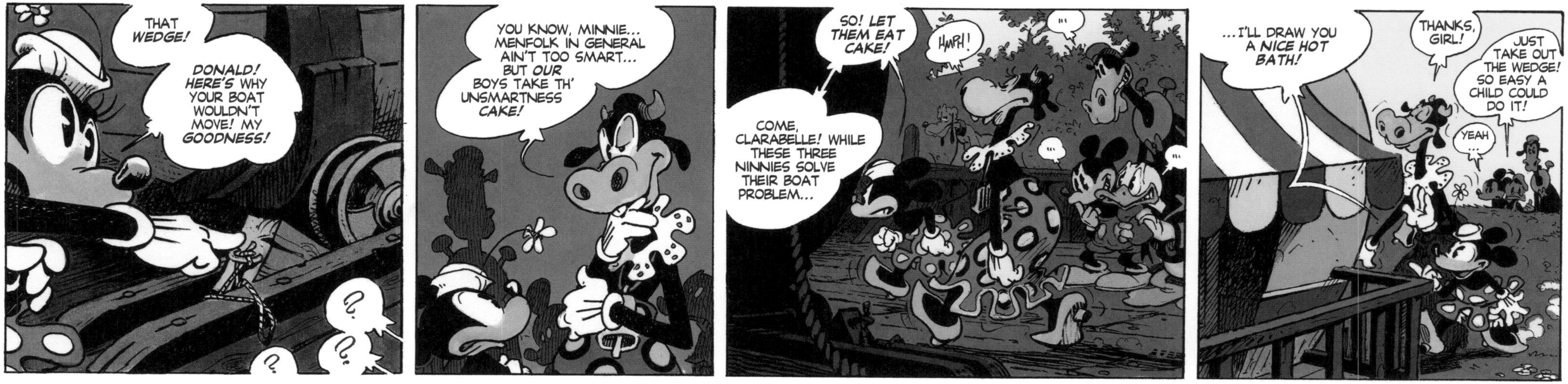
THAT *WEDGE!*
DONALD! HERE'S WHY YOUR BOAT WOULDN'T MOVE! MY *GOODNESS!*
?
?
?
YOU KNOW, MINNIE... MENFOLK IN GENERAL AIN'T TOO SMART... BUT *OUR* BOYS TAKE TH' UNSMARTNESS *CAKE!*
COME, CLARABELLE! WHILE THESE THREE NINNIES SOLVE THEIR BOAT PROBLEM...
SO! *LET THEM EAT CAKE!*
HMPH!
...I'LL DRAW YOU A *NICE HOT BATH!*
THANKS, GIRL!
JUST TAKE OUT THE WEDGE! SO EASY A CHILD COULD DO IT!
YEAH ...

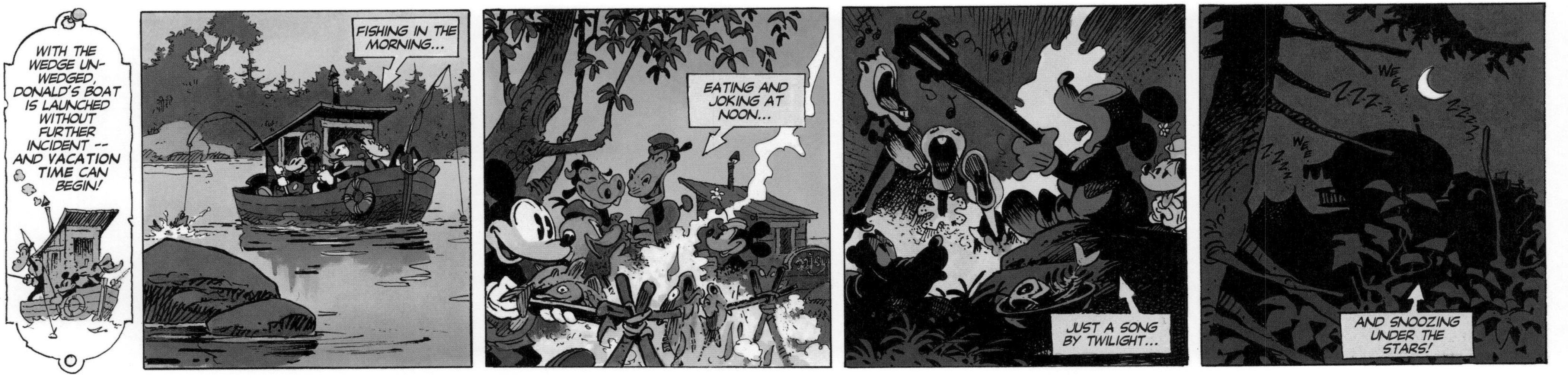
WITH THE WEDGE UN-WEDGED, DONALD'S BOAT IS LAUNCHED WITHOUT FURTHER INCIDENT -- AND VACATION TIME CAN BEGIN!
FISHING IN THE MORNING...
EATING AND JOKING AT NOON...
JUST A SONG BY TWILIGHT...
AND SNOOZING UNDER THE STARS!

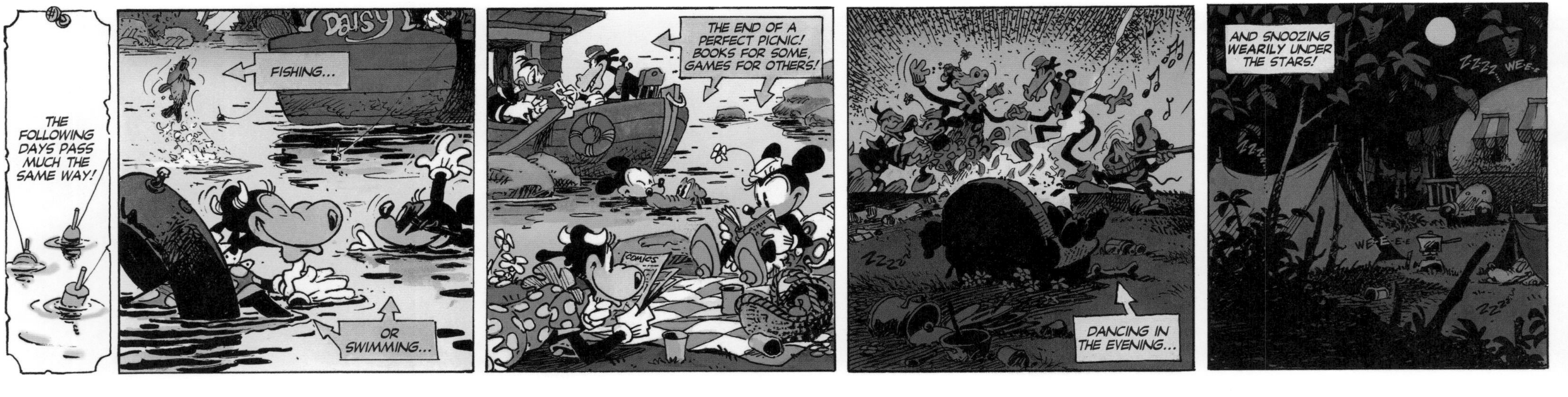
THE FOLLOWING DAYS PASS MUCH THE SAME WAY!
FISHING...
OR SWIMMING...
THE END OF A PERFECT PICNIC! BOOKS FOR SOME, GAMES FOR OTHERS!
COMICS
DANCING IN THE EVENING...
AND SNOOZING WEARILY UNDER THE STARS!

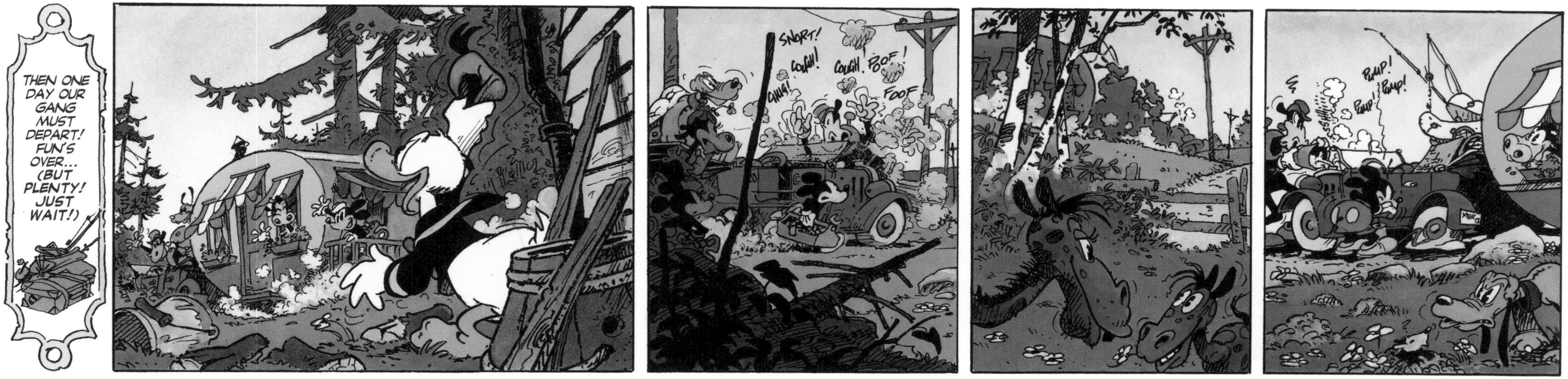
THEN ONE DAY OUR GANG MUST DEPART! FUN'S OVER... (BUT PLENTY! JUST WAIT!)
SNORT!
COUGH!
CHUG!
COUGH. POOF!
FOOF
SSSHHH
PUMP!
PUMP!
PUMP!

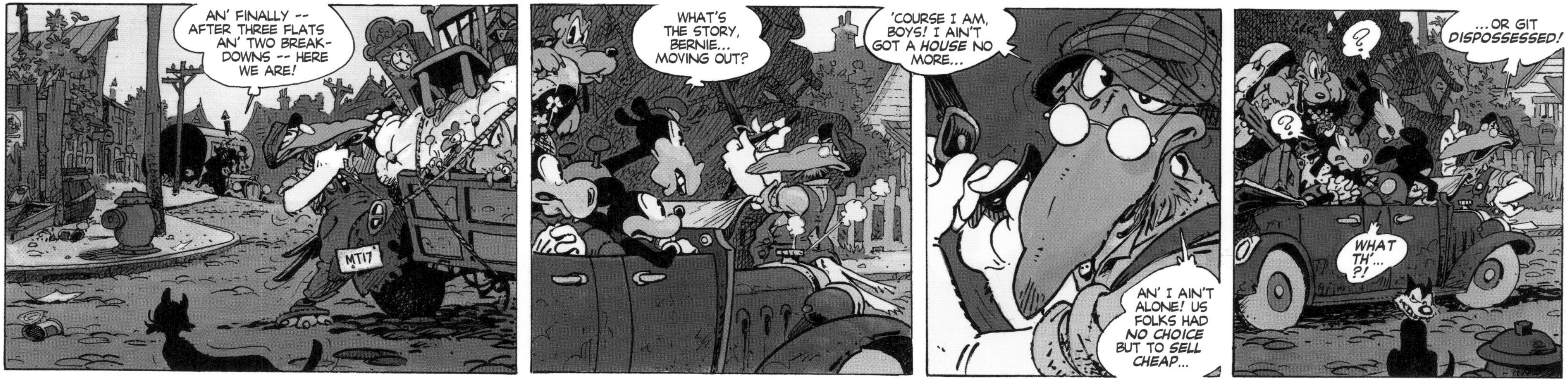
AN' FINALLY -- AFTER THREE FLATS AN' TWO BREAK-DOWNS -- HERE WE ARE!
MT17
WHAT'S THE STORY, BERNIE... MOVING OUT?
'COURSE I AM, BOYS! I AIN'T GOT A *HOUSE* NO MORE...
AN' I AIN'T ALONE! US FOLKS HAD *NO CHOICE* BUT TO *SELL CHEAP*...
...OR GIT *DISPOSSESSED!*
?
?
WHAT TH'... ?!

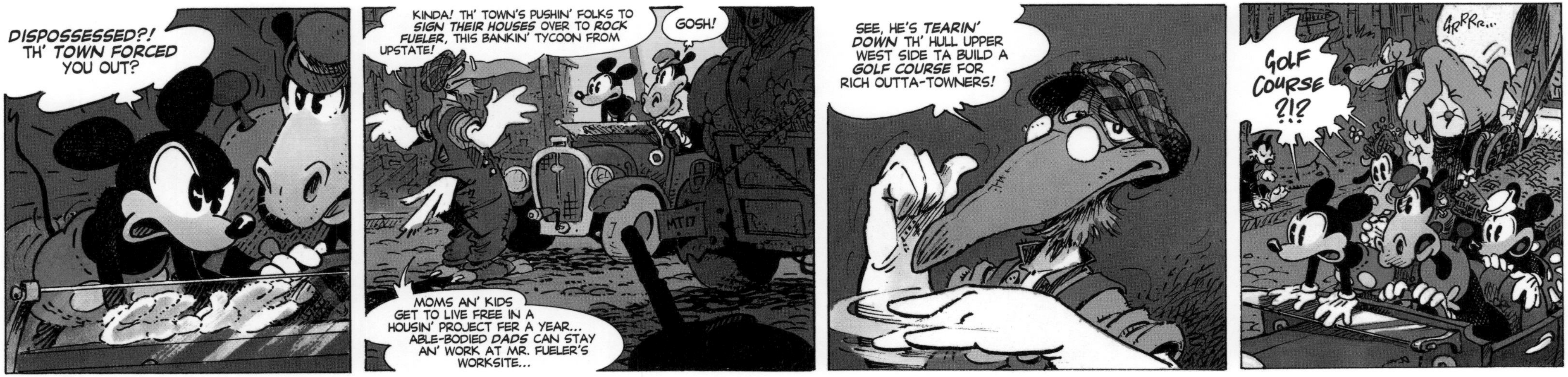
DISPOSSESSED?! TH' TOWN FORCED YOU OUT?
KINDA! TH' TOWN'S PUSHIN' FOLKS TO SIGN THEIR HOUSES OVER TO ROCK FUELER, THIS BANKIN' TYCOON FROM UPSTATE!
GOSH!
MOMS AN' KIDS GET TO LIVE FREE IN A HOUSIN' PROJECT FER A YEAR... ABLE-BODIED DADS CAN STAY AN' WORK AT MR. FUELER'S WORKSITE...
SEE, HE'S TEARIN' DOWN TH' HULL UPPER WEST SIDE TA BUILD A GOLF COURSE FOR RICH OUTTA-TOWNERS!
GRRRR...
GOLF COURSE ?!?

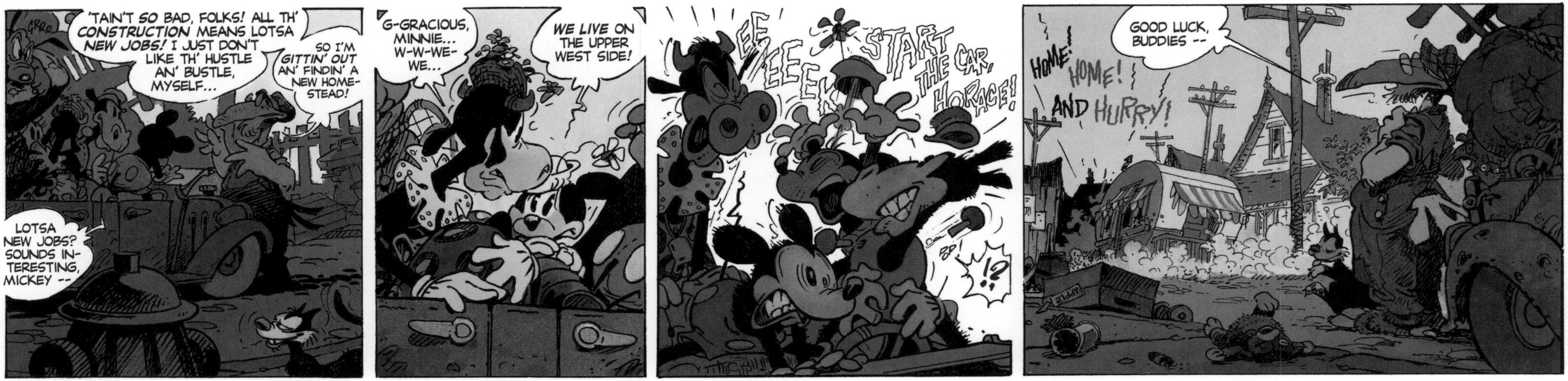
'TAIN'T SO BAD, FOLKS! ALL TH' CONSTRUCTION MEANS LOTSA NEW JOBS! I JUST DON'T LIKE TH' HUSTLE AN' BUSTLE, MYSELF...
SO I'M GITTIN' OUT AN' FINDIN' A NEW HOMESTEAD!
LOTSA NEW JOBS? SOUNDS INTERESTING, MICKEY --
G-GRACIOUS, MINNIE... W-W-WE-WE...
WE LIVE ON THE UPPER WEST SIDE!
EEEEEEK!
START THE CAR, HORACE!
!?
GOOD LUCK, BUDDIES --
HOME! HOME! AND HURRY!

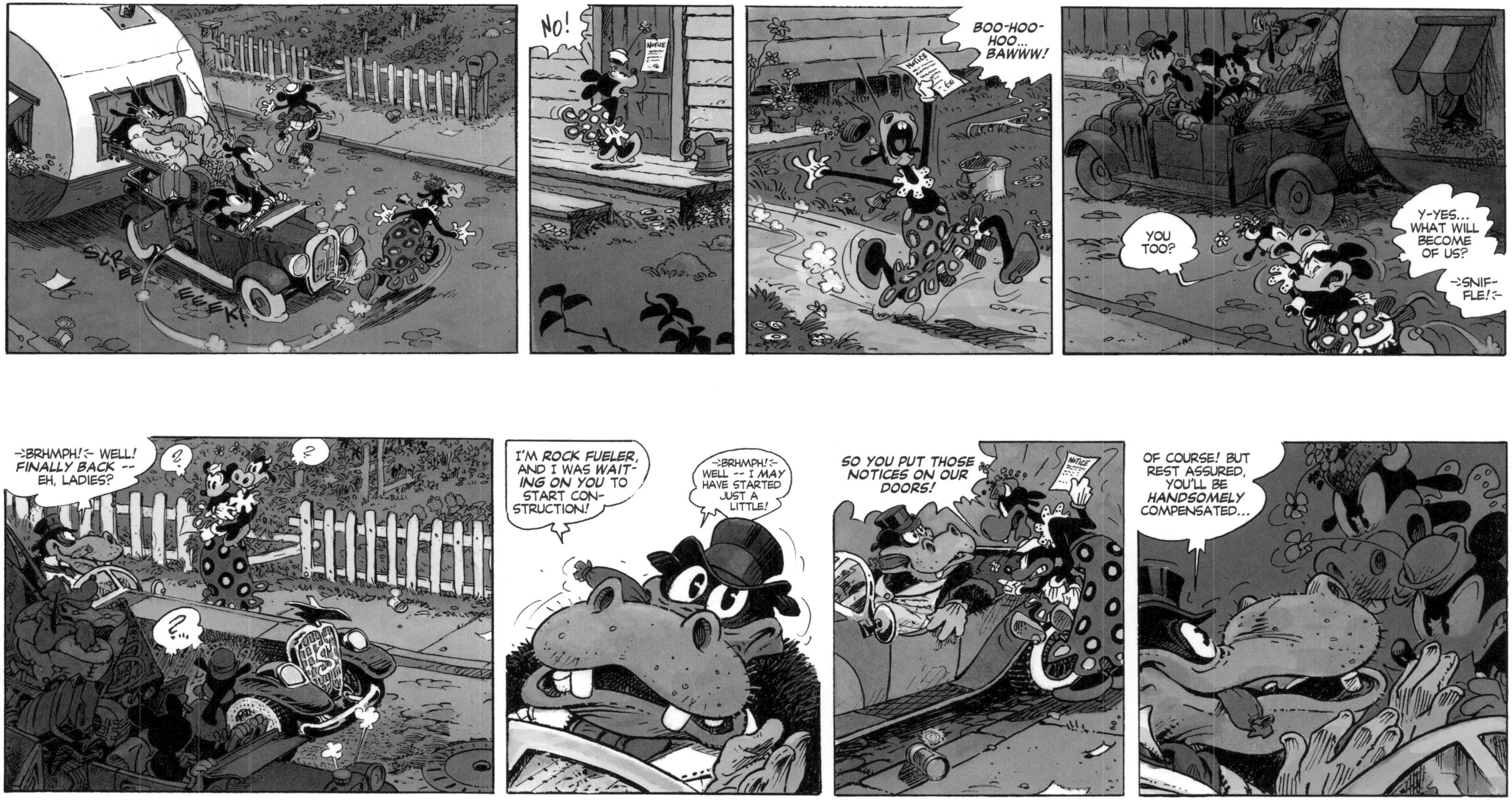
SCREE
EEEK!
NO!
BOO-HOO-HOO... BAWWW!
YOU TOO?
Y-YES... WHAT WILL BECOME OF US?
-SNIF-FLE!-
-BRHMPH!- WELL! FINALLY BACK -- EH, LADIES?
?
?
?!...
I'M ROCK FUELER, AND I WAS WAITING ON YOU TO START CONSTRUCTION!
-BRHMPH!- WELL -- I MAY HAVE STARTED JUST A LITTLE!
SO YOU PUT THOSE NOTICES ON OUR DOORS!
OF COURSE! BUT REST ASSURED, YOU'LL BE HANDSOMELY COMPENSATED...

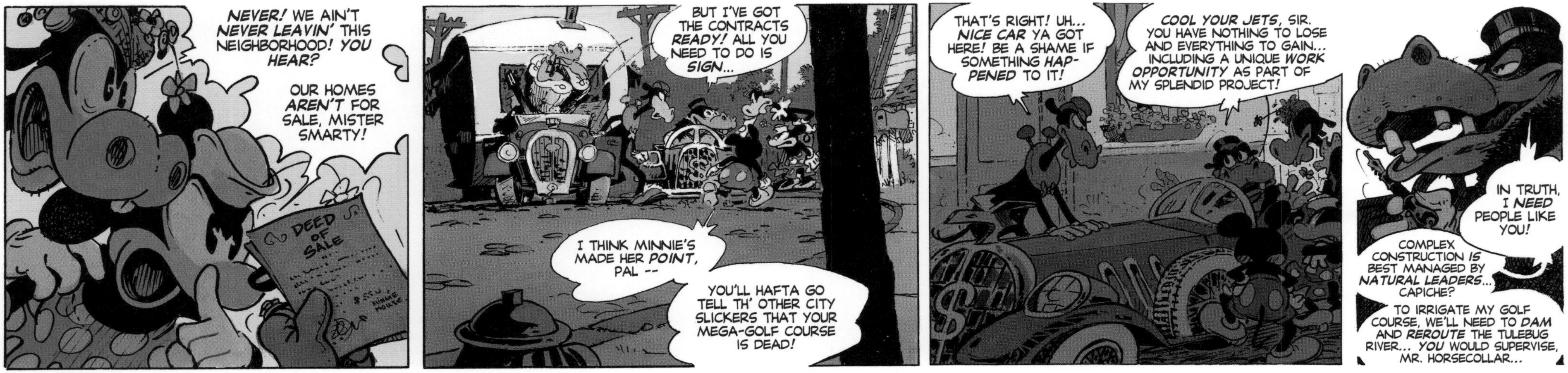
NEVER! WE AIN'T NEVER LEAVIN' THIS NEIGHBORHOOD! YOU HEAR?
OUR HOMES AREN'T FOR SALE, MISTER SMARTY!
DEED OF SALE
MINNIE MOUSE
BUT I'VE GOT THE CONTRACTS READY! ALL YOU NEED TO DO IS SIGN...
I THINK MINNIE'S MADE HER POINT, PAL --
YOU'LL HAFTA GO TELL TH' OTHER CITY SLICKERS THAT YOUR MEGA-GOLF COURSE IS DEAD!
THAT'S RIGHT! UH... NICE CAR YA GOT HERE! BE A SHAME IF SOMETHING HAPPENED TO IT!
COOL YOUR JETS, SIR. YOU HAVE NOTHING TO LOSE AND EVERYTHING TO GAIN... INCLUDING A UNIQUE WORK OPPORTUNITY AS PART OF MY SPLENDID PROJECT!
IN TRUTH, I NEED PEOPLE LIKE YOU!
COMPLEX CONSTRUCTION IS BEST MANAGED BY NATURAL LEADERS... CAPICHE?
TO IRRIGATE MY GOLF COURSE, WE'LL NEED TO DAM AND REROUTE THE TULEBUG RIVER... YOU WOULD SUPERVISE, MR. HORSECOLLAR...

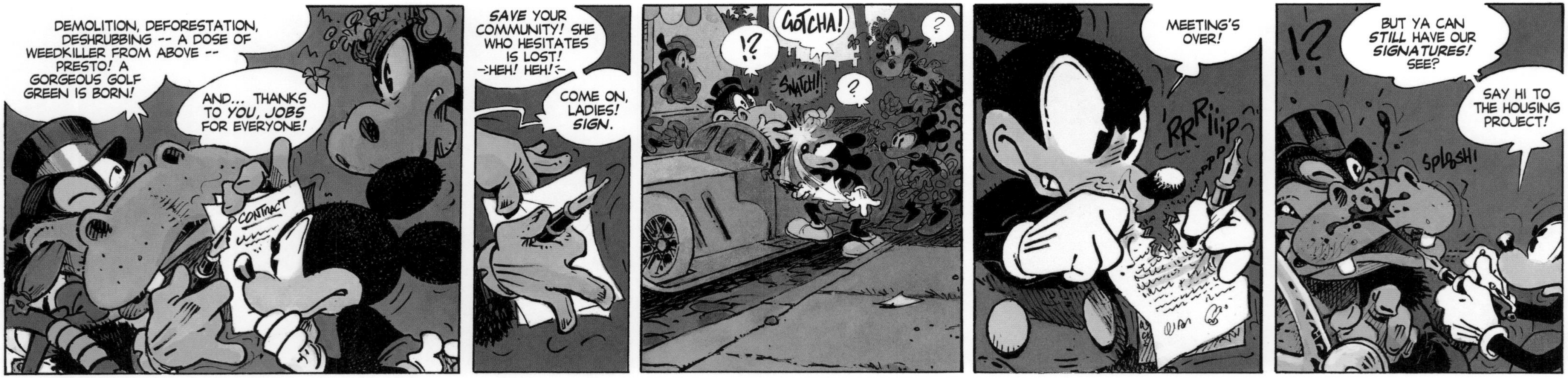
DEMOLITION, DEFORESTATION, DESHRUBBING -- A DOSE OF WEEDKILLER FROM ABOVE -- PRESTO! A GORGEOUS GOLF GREEN IS BORN!
AND... THANKS TO YOU, JOBS FOR EVERYONE!
CONTRACT
SAVE YOUR COMMUNITY! SHE WHO HESITATES IS LOST! HEH! HEH!
COME ON, LADIES! SIGN.
!?
GOTCHA!
?
SNATCH!
?
MEETING'S OVER!
RRRIIIP
!?
BUT YA CAN STILL HAVE OUR SIGNATURES! SEE?
SAY HI TO THE HOUSING PROJECT!
SPLOOSH!

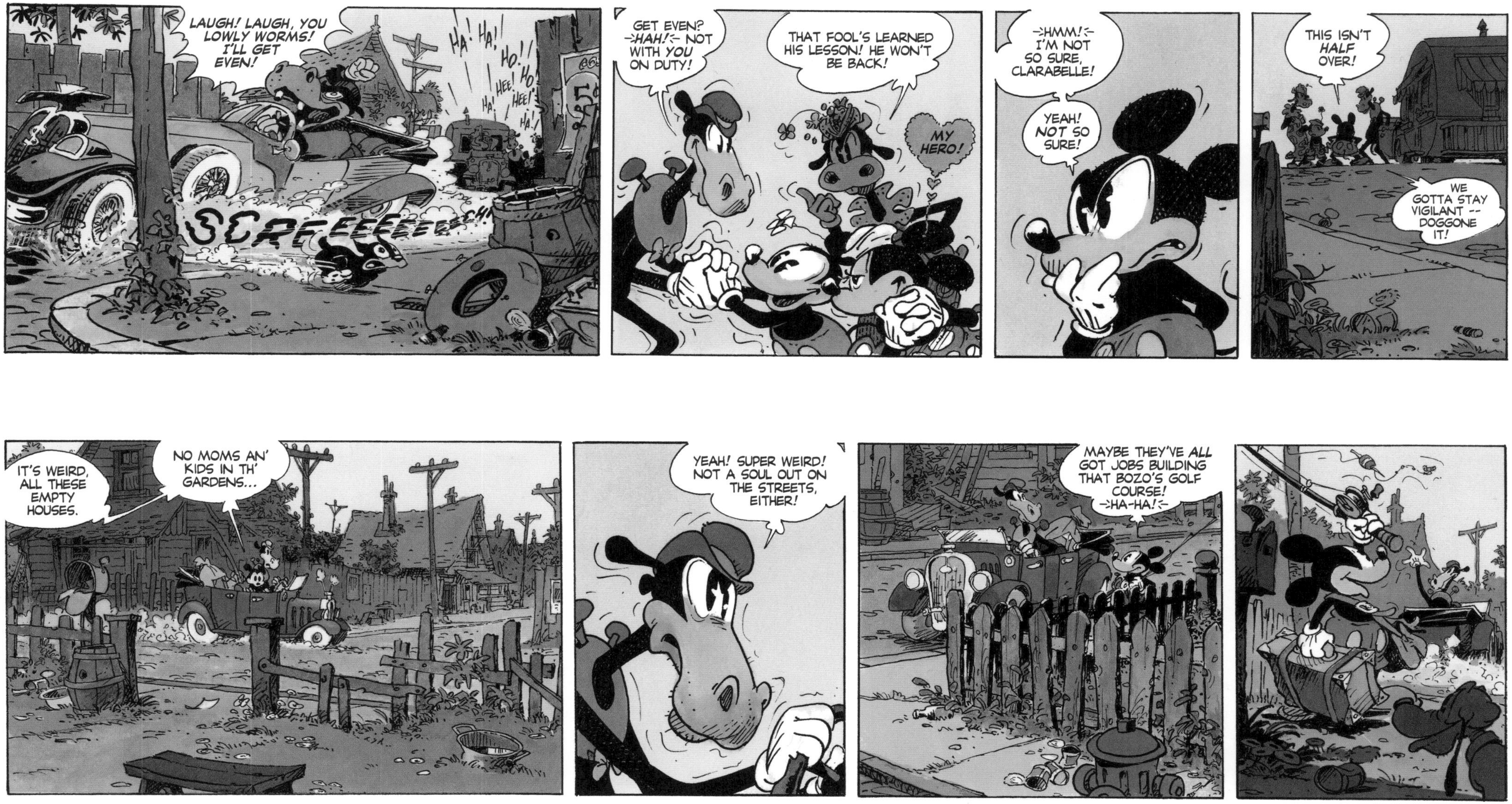
LAUGH! LAUGH, YOU LOWLY WORMS! I'LL GET EVEN!
HA! HA! HO! HO! HEE! HEE! HA! HA!
GET EVEN? -HAH!- NOT WITH YOU ON DUTY!
THAT FOOL'S LEARNED HIS LESSON! HE WON'T BE BACK!
MY HERO!
-HMM!- I'M NOT SO SURE, CLARABELLE!
YEAH! NOT SO SURE!
THIS ISN'T HALF OVER!
WE GOTTA STAY VIGILANT -- DOGGONE IT!
IT'S WEIRD, ALL THESE EMPTY HOUSES.
NO MOMS AN' KIDS IN TH' GARDENS...
YEAH! SUPER WEIRD! NOT A SOUL OUT ON THE STREETS, EITHER!
MAYBE THEY'VE ALL GOT JOBS BUILDING THAT BOZO'S GOLF COURSE! -HA-HA!-

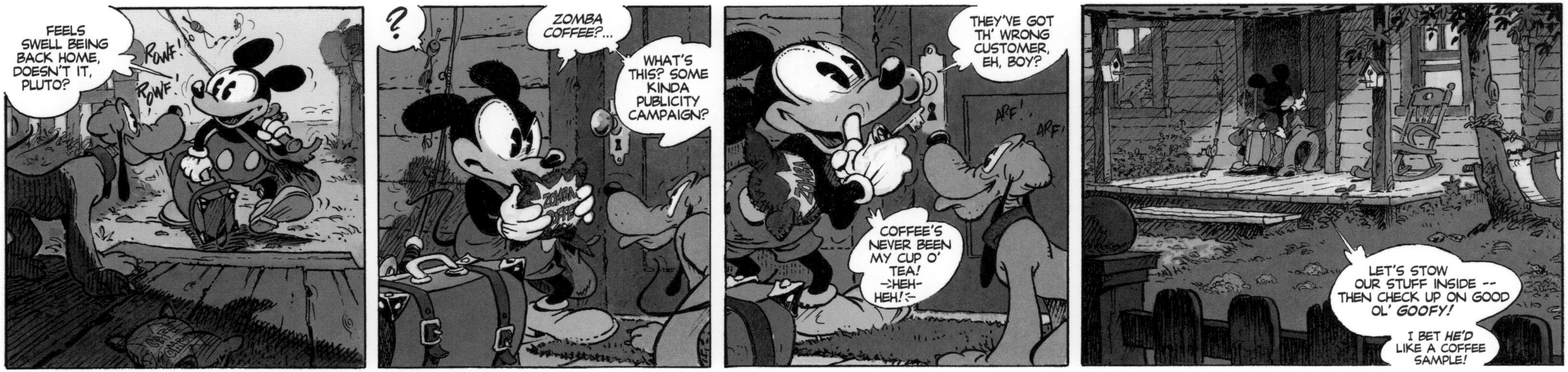
FEELS SWELL BEING BACK HOME, DOESN'T IT, PLUTO?
ROWF!
ROWF!
?
ZOMBA COFFEE?...
WHAT'S THIS? SOME KINDA PUBLICITY CAMPAIGN?
THEY'VE GOT TH' WRONG CUSTOMER, EH, BOY?
ARF!
ARF!
COFFEE'S NEVER BEEN MY CUP O' TEA! –HEH-HEH!–
LET'S STOW OUR STUFF INSIDE -- THEN CHECK UP ON GOOD OL' GOOFY!
I BET HE'D LIKE A COFFEE SAMPLE!

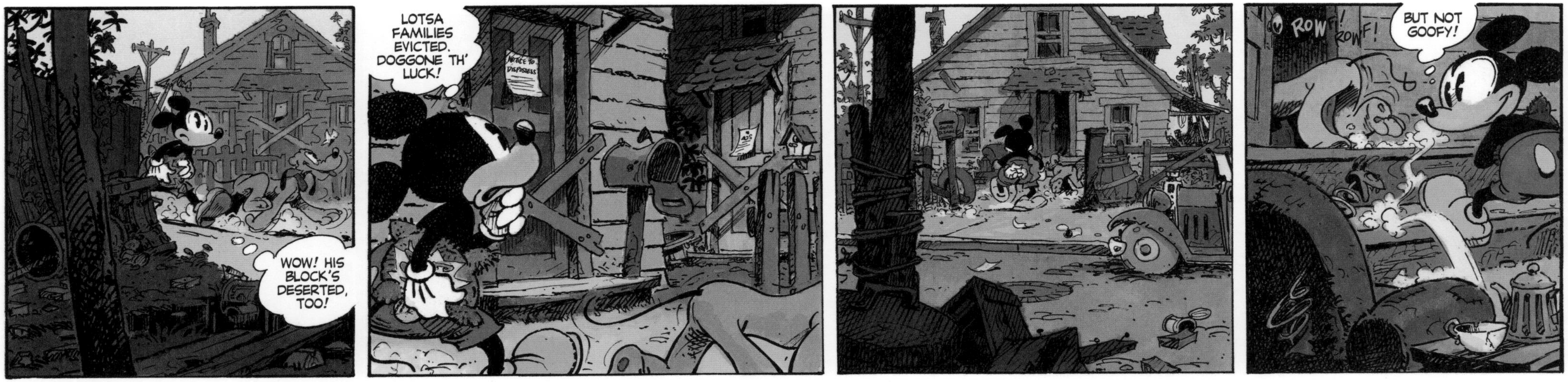
WOW! HIS BLOCK'S DESERTED, TOO!
LOTSA FAMILIES EVICTED. DOGGONE TH' LUCK!
ROWF!
ROWF!
BUT NOT GOOFY!

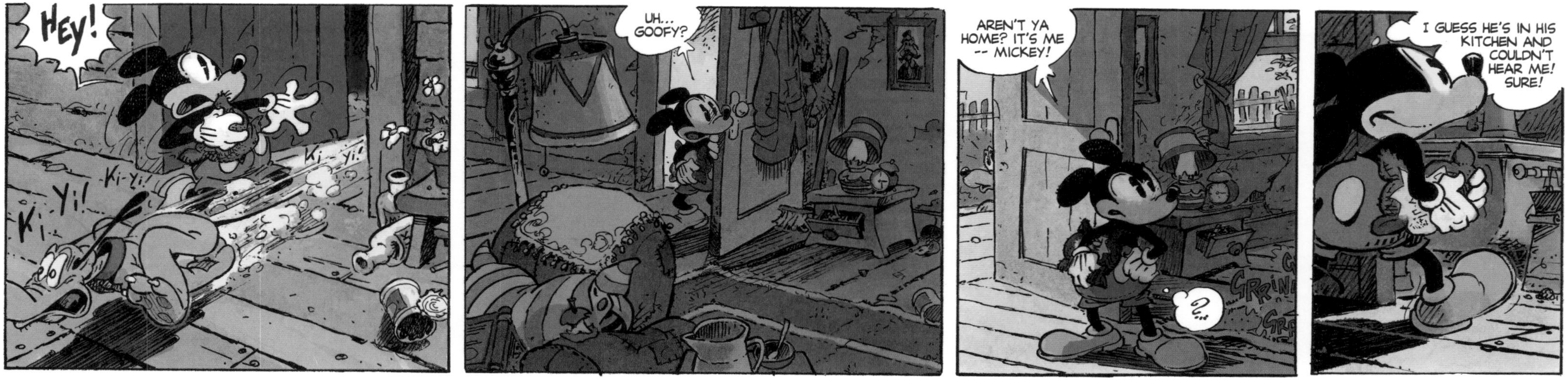
HEY!
KI-YI!
KI-YI!
KI
YI!
UH... GOOFY?
AREN'T YA HOME? IT'S ME -- MICKEY!
I GUESS HE'S IN HIS KITCHEN AND COULDN'T HEAR ME! SURE!

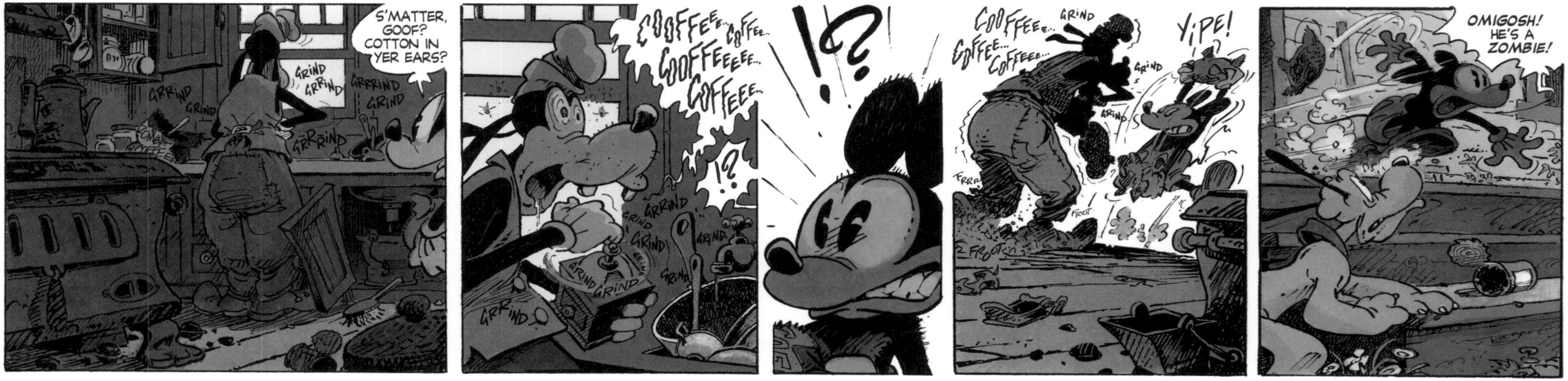
S'MATTER, GOOF? COTTON IN YER EARS?
GRIND GRRIND
GRRRIND GRIND
GRRRIND
COOFFEEE... COFFEE..
GOOFFEEEEE...
COFFEEE...
!?
!?
COOFFEEE...
COFFEE...
COFFEEE...
YIPE!
OMIGOSH! HE'S A ZOMBIE!

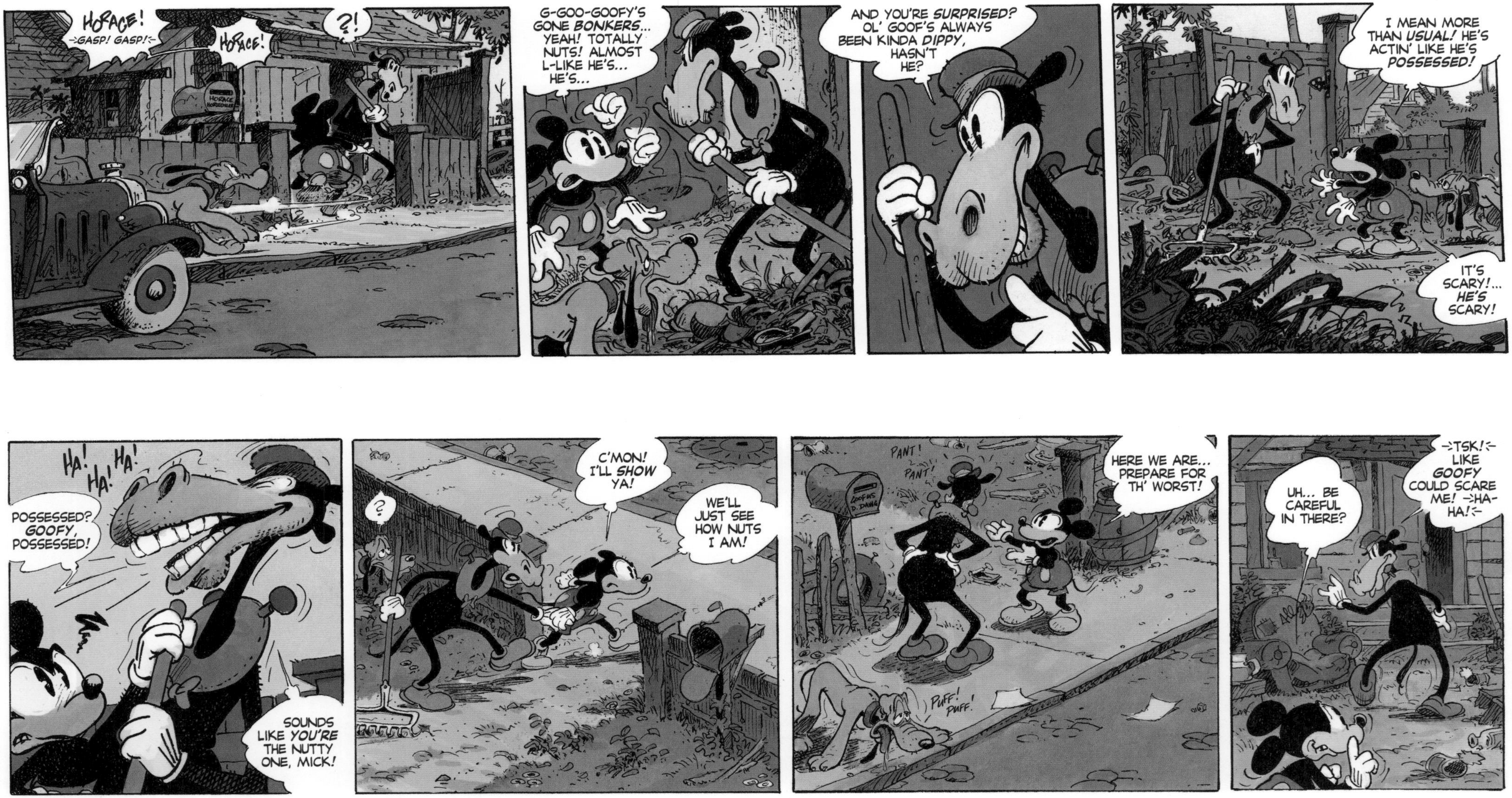

HORACE!
-GASP! GASP!-
HORACE!
?!
G-GOO-GOOFY'S GONE *BONKERS*... YEAH! TOTALLY NUTS! ALMOST L-LIKE HE'S... HE'S...
AND YOU'RE *SURPRISED?* OL' GOOF'S ALWAYS BEEN KINDA *DIPPY*, HASN'T HE?
I MEAN MORE THAN *USUAL!* HE'S ACTIN' LIKE HE'S *POSSESSED!*
IT'S SCARY!... *HE'S* SCARY!
HA! HA! HA!
POSSESSED? *GOOFY*, POSSESSED!
SOUNDS LIKE *YOU'RE* THE NUTTY ONE, MICK!
?
C'MON! I'LL *SHOW* YA!
WE'LL JUST SEE HOW NUTS I AM!
PANT! PANT!
PUFF! PUFF!
HERE WE ARE... PREPARE FOR TH' WORST!
UH... BE CAREFUL IN THERE?
-TSK!- LIKE *GOOFY* COULD SCARE ME! -HA-HA!-

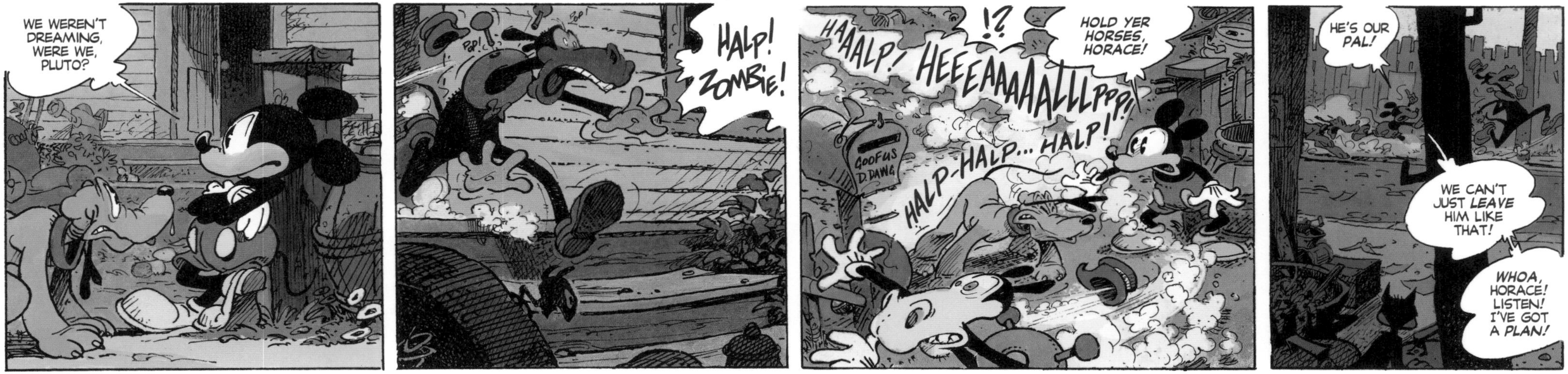
WE WEREN'T DREAMING, WERE WE, PLUTO?
HALP! ZOMBIE!
HAAALP! HEEEAAAAAALLLPPP!
!?
HOLD YER HORSES, HORACE!
GOOFUS D.DAWG
HALP-HALP... HALP!
HE'S OUR PAL!
WE CAN'T JUST LEAVE HIM LIKE THAT!
WHOA, HORACE! LISTEN! I'VE GOT A PLAN!

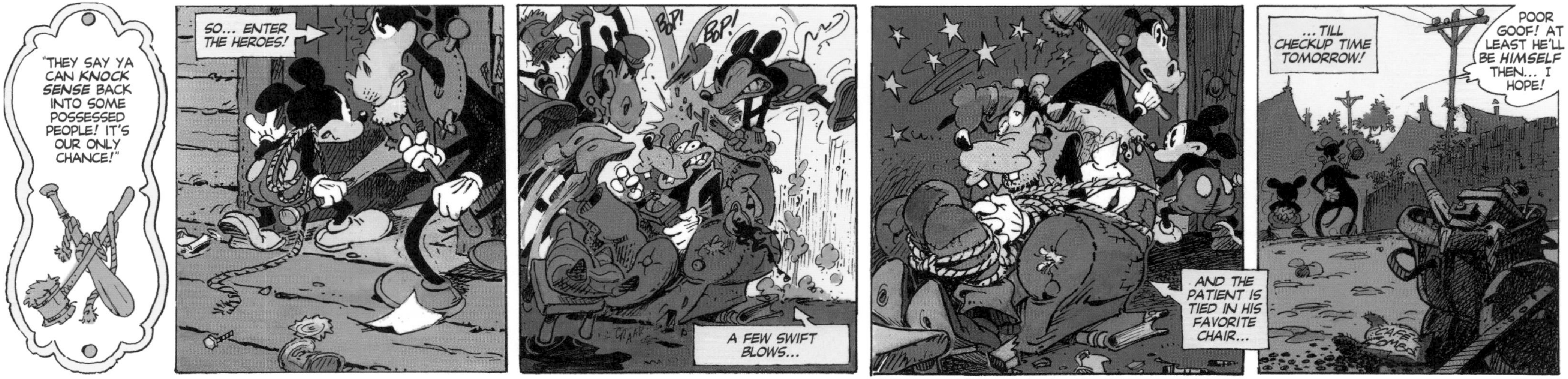
"THEY SAY YA CAN KNOCK SENSE BACK INTO SOME POSSESSED PEOPLE! IT'S OUR ONLY CHANCE!"
SO... ENTER THE HEROES!
BOP!
BOP!
A FEW SWIFT BLOWS...
AND THE PATIENT IS TIED IN HIS FAVORITE CHAIR...
...TILL CHECKUP TIME TOMORROW!
POOR GOOF! AT LEAST HE'LL BE HIMSELF THEN... I HOPE!

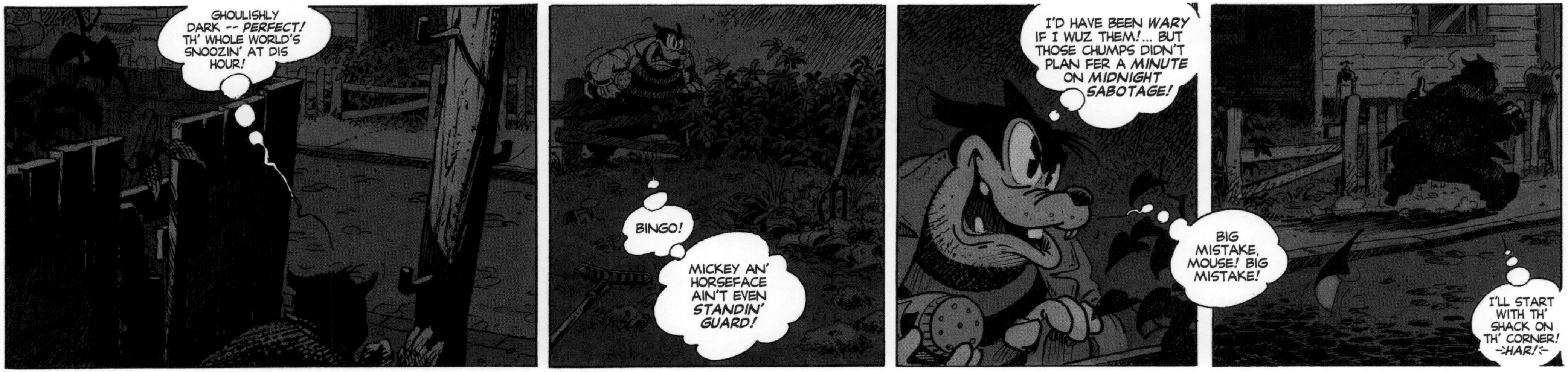
GHOULISHLY DARK -- PERFECT! TH' WHOLE WORLD'S SNOOZIN' AT DIS HOUR!
BINGO!
MICKEY AN' HORSEFACE AIN'T EVEN STANDIN' GUARD!
I'D HAVE BEEN WARY IF I WUZ THEM!... BUT THOSE CHUMPS DIDN'T PLAN FER A MINUTE ON MIDNIGHT SABOTAGE!
BIG MISTAKE, MOUSE! BIG MISTAKE!
I'LL START WITH TH' SHACK ON TH' CORNER! -HAR!-

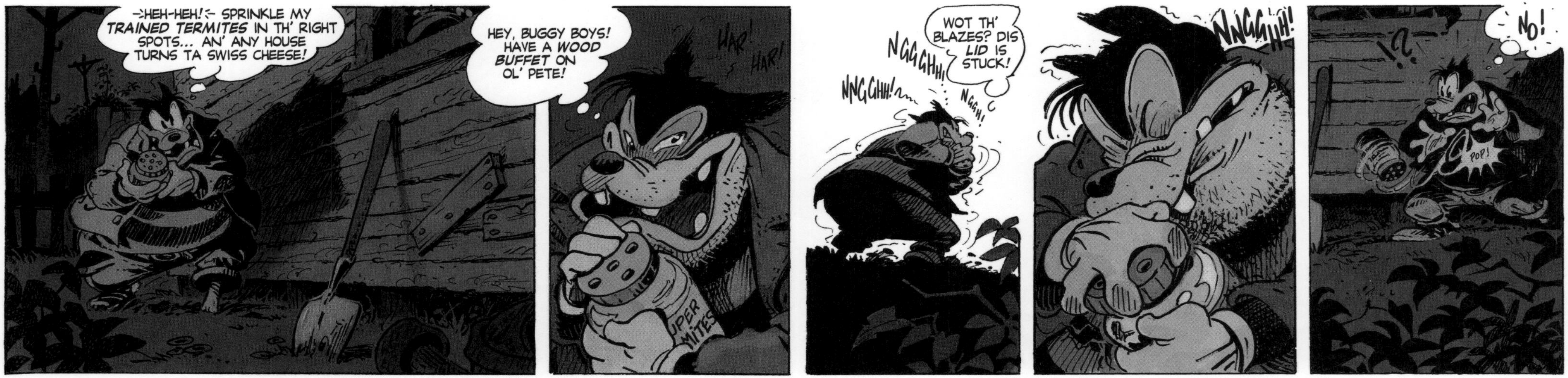
-HEH-HEH!- SPRINKLE MY TRAINED TERMITES IN TH' RIGHT SPOTS... AN' ANY HOUSE TURNS TA SWISS CHEESE!
HEY, BUGGY BOYS! HAVE A WOOD BUFFET ON OL' PETE!
HAR! HAR!
WOT TH' BLAZES? DIS LID IS STUCK!
NNGGHH!
NGGGHH!
NGGH!
NNGGHH!
!?
NO!
POP!

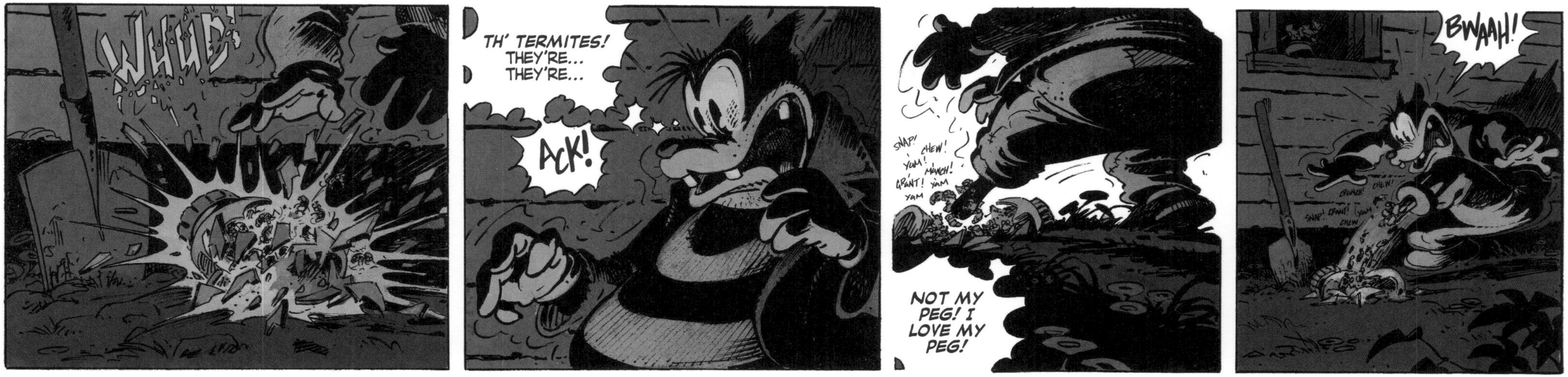
WHUD!
TH' TERMITES! THEY'RE... THEY'RE...
ACK!
NOT MY PEG! I LOVE MY PEG!
BWAAH!

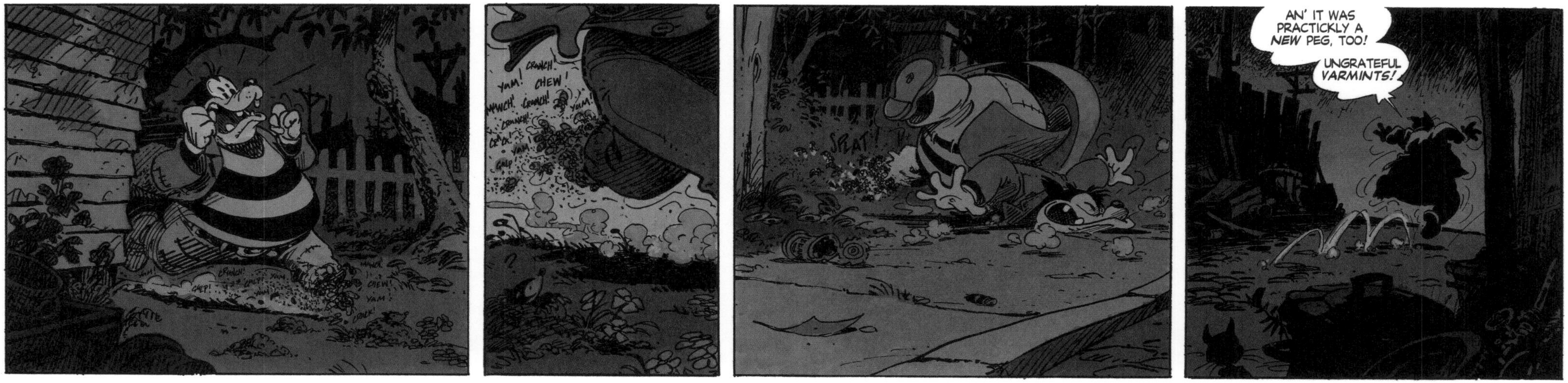
SPLAT!
AN' IT WAS PRACTICKLY A NEW PEG, TOO!
UNGRATEFUL VARMINTS!

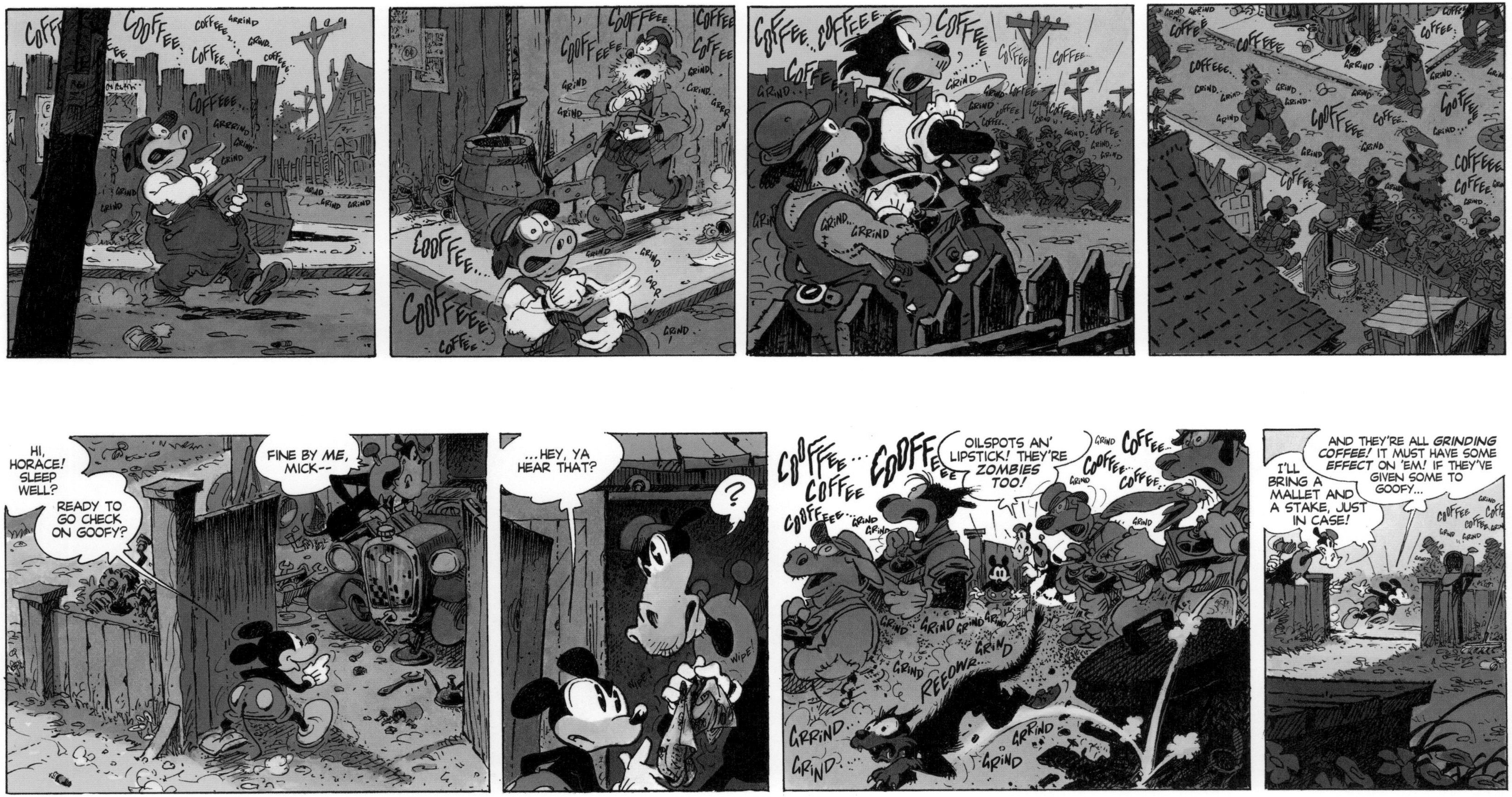
COFFEE
GRIND
HI, HORACE! SLEEP WELL?
READY TO GO CHECK ON GOOFY?
FINE BY ME, MICK--
...HEY, YA HEAR THAT?
?
WIPE!
OILSPOTS AN' LIPSTICK! THEY'RE ZOMBIES TOO!
REEOWR
AND THEY'RE ALL GRINDING COFFEE! IT MUST HAVE SOME EFFECT ON 'EM! IF THEY'VE GIVEN SOME TO GOOFY...
I'LL BRING A MALLET AND A STAKE, JUST IN CASE!

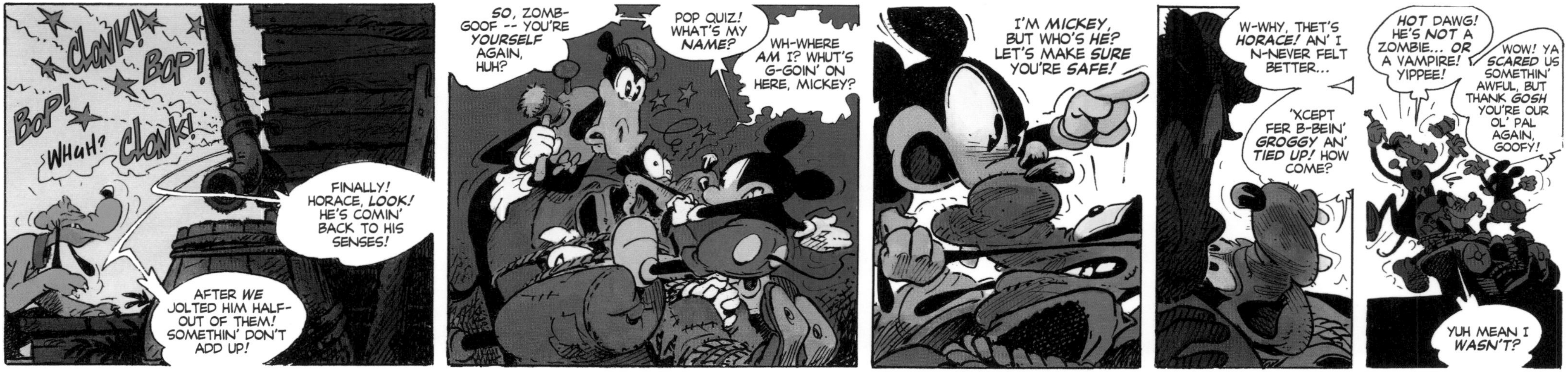

CLONK!
BOP!
BOP!
WHUH?
CLONK!
FINALLY! HORACE, LOOK! HE'S COMIN' BACK TO HIS SENSES!
AFTER WE JOLTED HIM HALF-OUT OF THEM! SOMETHIN' DON'T ADD UP!
SO, ZOMB-GOOF -- YOU'RE YOURSELF AGAIN, HUH?
POP QUIZ! WHAT'S MY NAME?
WH-WHERE AM I? WHUT'S G-GOIN' ON HERE, MICKEY?
I'M MICKEY, BUT WHO'S HE? LET'S MAKE SURE YOU'RE SAFE!
W-WHY, THET'S HORACE! AN' I N-NEVER FELT BETTER...
'XCEPT FER B-BEIN' GROGGY AN' TIED UP! HOW COME?
HOT DAWG! HE'S NOT A ZOMBIE... OR A VAMPIRE! YIPPEE!
WOW! YA SCARED US SOMETHIN' AWFUL, BUT THANK GOSH YOU'RE OUR OL' PAL AGAIN, GOOFY!
YUH MEAN I WASN'T?

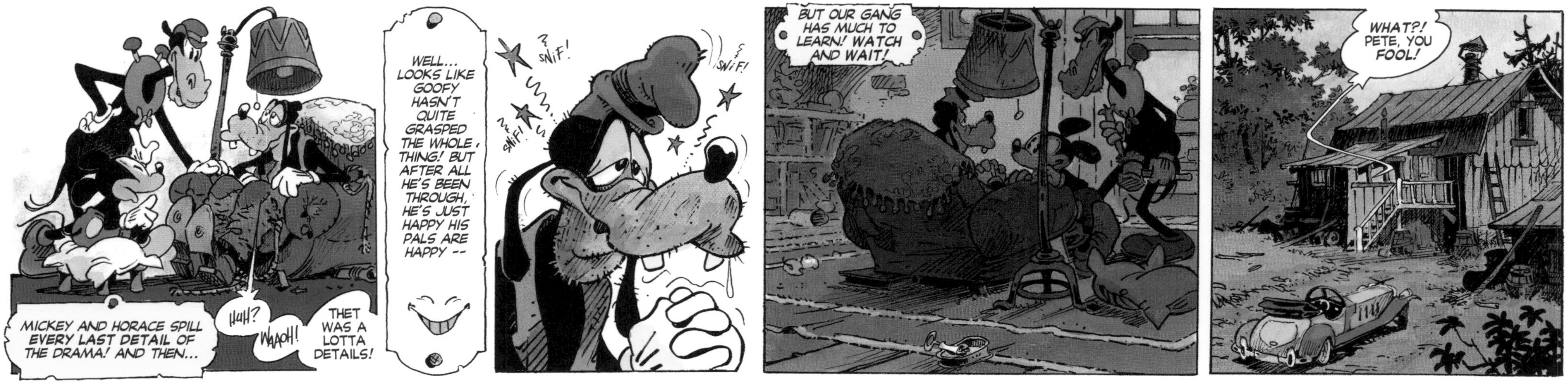

MICKEY AND HORACE SPILL EVERY LAST DETAIL OF THE DRAMA! AND THEN...
HUH?
WAAOH!
THET WAS A LOTTA DETAILS!
WELL... LOOKS LIKE GOOFY HASN'T QUITE GRASPED THE WHOLE THING! BUT AFTER ALL HE'S BEEN THROUGH, HE'S JUST HAPPY HIS PALS ARE HAPPY --
SNIF!
SNIF!
SNIF!
BUT OUR GANG HAS MUCH TO LEARN! WATCH AND WAIT!
WHAT?! PETE, YOU FOOL!

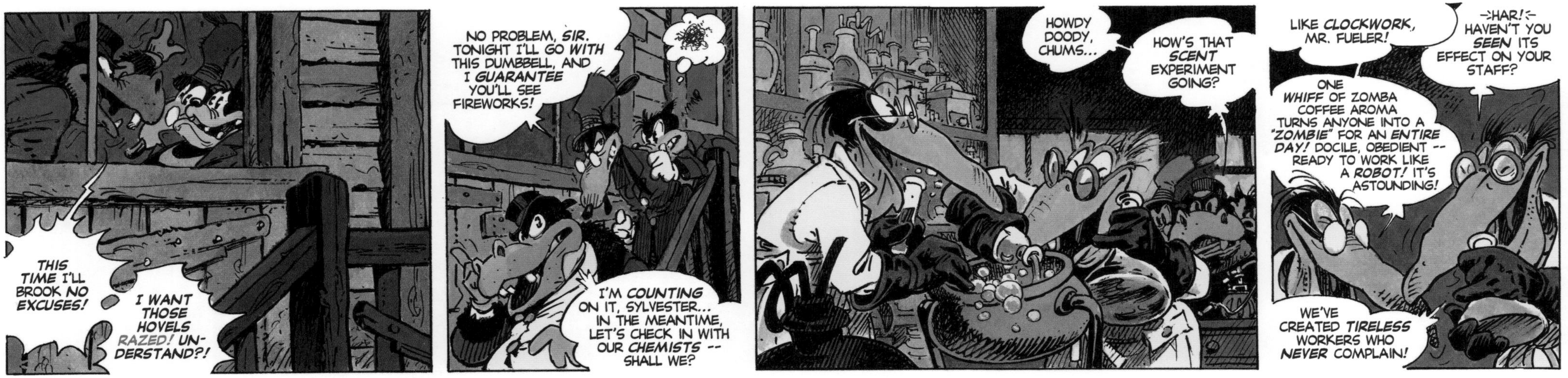
THIS TIME I'LL BROOK NO EXCUSES!
I WANT THOSE HOVELS RAZED! UNDERSTAND?!
NO PROBLEM, SIR. TONIGHT I'LL GO WITH THIS DUMBBELL, AND I GUARANTEE YOU'LL SEE FIREWORKS!
I'M COUNTING ON IT, SYLVESTER... IN THE MEANTIME, LET'S CHECK IN WITH OUR CHEMISTS -- SHALL WE?
HOWDY DOODY, CHUMS...
HOW'S THAT SCENT EXPERIMENT GOING?
LIKE CLOCKWORK, MR. FUELER!
ONE WHIFF OF ZOMBA COFFEE AROMA TURNS ANYONE INTO A "ZOMBIE" FOR AN ENTIRE DAY! DOCILE, OBEDIENT -- READY TO WORK LIKE A ROBOT! IT'S ASTOUNDING!
-HAR!- HAVEN'T YOU SEEN ITS EFFECT ON YOUR STAFF?
WE'VE CREATED TIRELESS WORKERS WHO NEVER COMPLAIN!

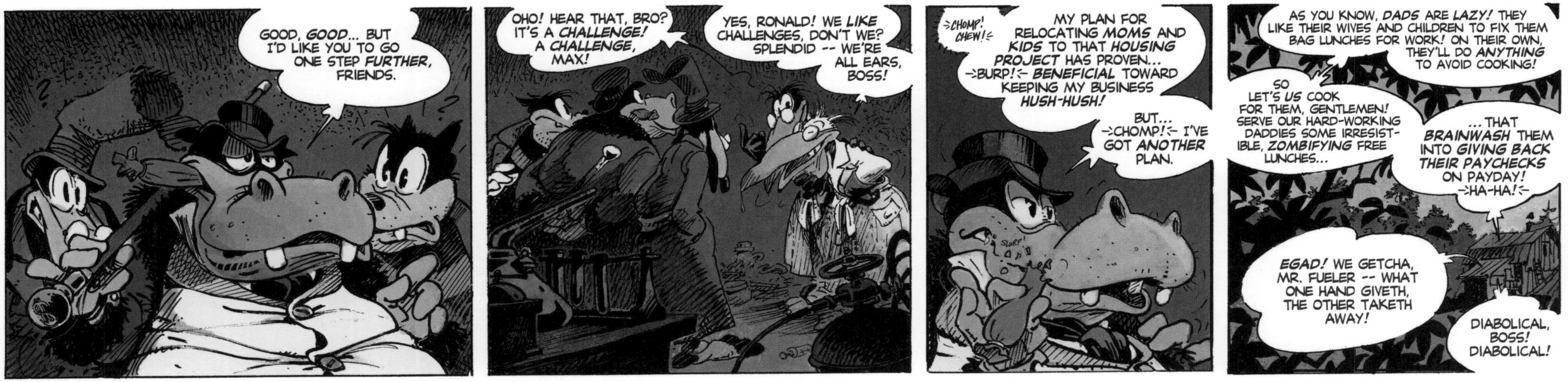
GOOD, GOOD... BUT I'D LIKE YOU TO GO ONE STEP FURTHER, FRIENDS.
OHO! HEAR THAT, BRO? IT'S A CHALLENGE! A CHALLENGE, MAX!
YES, RONALD! WE LIKE CHALLENGES, DON'T WE? SPLENDID -- WE'RE ALL EARS, BOSS!
-CHOMP! CHEW!-
MY PLAN FOR RELOCATING MOMS AND KIDS TO THAT HOUSING PROJECT HAS PROVEN... -BURP!- BENEFICIAL TOWARD KEEPING MY BUSINESS HUSH-HUSH!
BUT... -CHOMP!- I'VE GOT ANOTHER PLAN.
SLURP!
AS YOU KNOW, DADS ARE LAZY! THEY LIKE THEIR WIVES AND CHILDREN TO FIX THEM BAG LUNCHES FOR WORK! ON THEIR OWN, THEY'LL DO ANYTHING TO AVOID COOKING!
SO LET'S US COOK FOR THEM, GENTLEMEN! SERVE OUR HARD-WORKING DADDIES SOME IRRESISTIBLE, ZOMBIFYING FREE LUNCHES...
...THAT BRAINWASH THEM INTO GIVING BACK THEIR PAYCHECKS ON PAYDAY! -HA-HA!-
EGAD! WE GETCHA, MR. FUELER -- WHAT ONE HAND GIVETH, THE OTHER TAKETH AWAY!
DIABOLICAL, BOSS! DIABOLICAL!

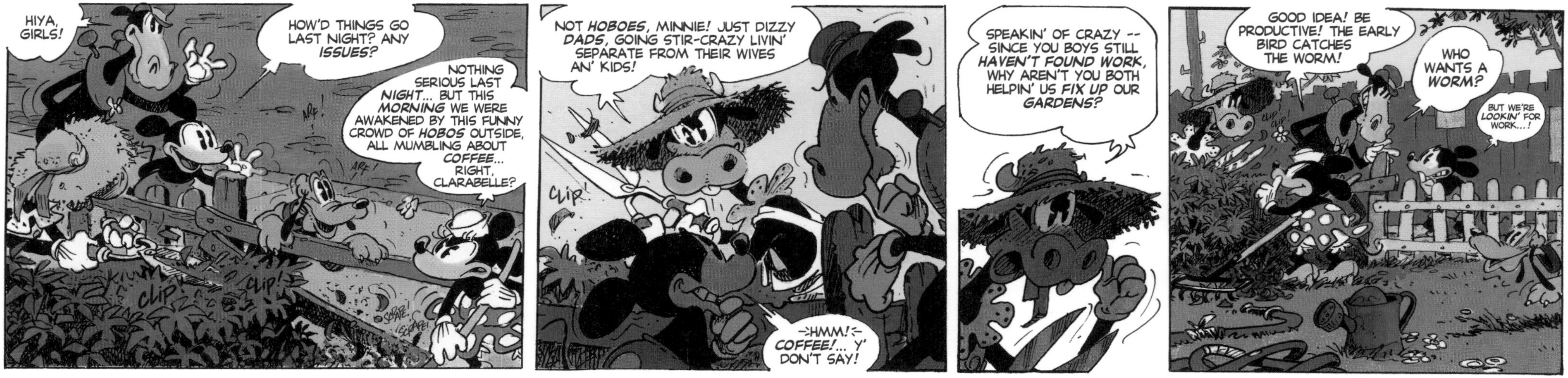
HIYA, GIRLS!
HOW'D THINGS GO LAST NIGHT? ANY ISSUES?
NOTHING SERIOUS LAST NIGHT... BUT THIS MORNING WE WERE AWAKENED BY THIS FUNNY CROWD OF HOBOS OUTSIDE, ALL MUMBLING ABOUT COFFEE... RIGHT, CLARABELLE?
CLIP
CLIP!
NOT HOBOES, MINNIE! JUST DIZZY DADS, GOING STIR-CRAZY LIVIN' SEPARATE FROM THEIR WIVES AN' KIDS!
CLIP!
HMM! COFFEE!... Y' DON'T SAY!
SPEAKIN' OF CRAZY -- SINCE YOU BOYS STILL HAVEN'T FOUND WORK, WHY AREN'T YOU BOTH HELPIN' US FIX UP OUR GARDENS?
GOOD IDEA! BE PRODUCTIVE! THE EARLY BIRD CATCHES THE WORM!
WHO WANTS A WORM?
BUT WE'RE LOOKIN' FOR WORK...!

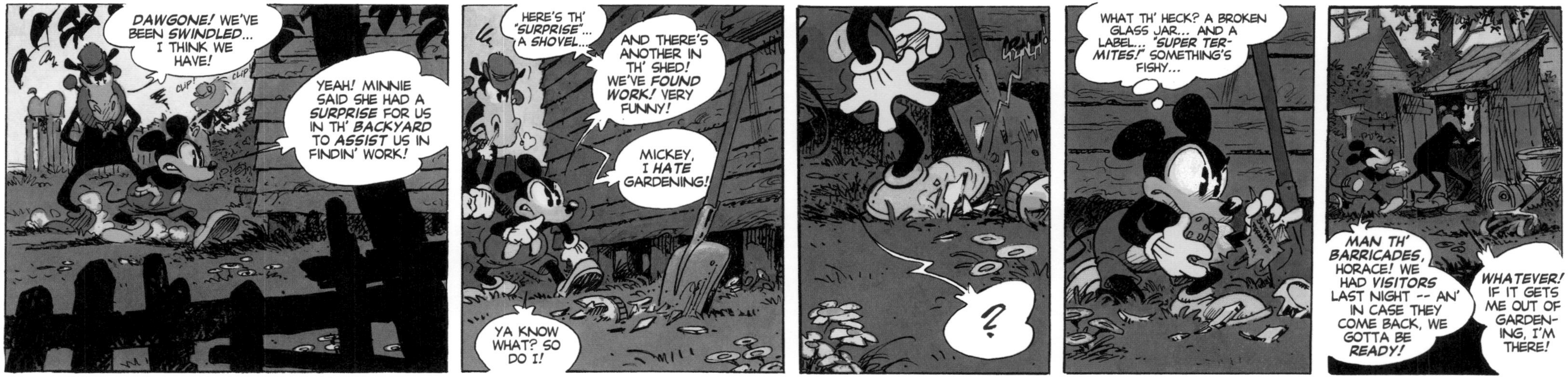
DAWGONE! WE'VE BEEN SWINDLED... I THINK WE HAVE!
YEAH! MINNIE SAID SHE HAD A SURPRISE FOR US IN TH' BACKYARD TO ASSIST US IN FINDIN' WORK!
HERE'S TH' "SURPRISE"... A SHOVEL...
AND THERE'S ANOTHER IN TH' SHED! WE'VE FOUND WORK! VERY FUNNY!
MICKEY, I HATE GARDENING!
YA KNOW WHAT? SO DO I!
?
WHAT TH' HECK? A BROKEN GLASS JAR... AND A LABEL... "SUPER TERMITES!" SOMETHING'S FISHY...
MAN TH' BARRICADES, HORACE! WE HAD VISITORS LAST NIGHT -- AN' IN CASE THEY COME BACK, WE GOTTA BE READY!
WHATEVER! IF IT GETS ME OUT OF GARDENING, I'M THERE!

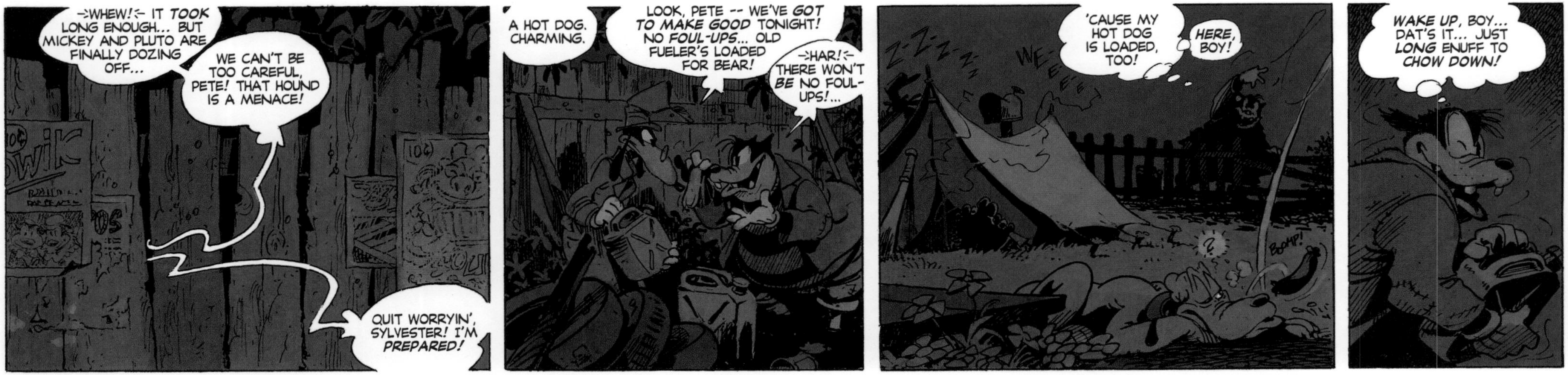

→WHEW!← IT TOOK LONG ENOUGH... BUT MICKEY AND PLUTO ARE FINALLY DOZING OFF...
WE CAN'T BE TOO CAREFUL, PETE! THAT HOUND IS A MENACE!
QUIT WORRYIN', SYLVESTER! I'M PREPARED!
A HOT DOG. CHARMING.
LOOK, PETE -- WE'VE GOT TO MAKE GOOD TONIGHT! NO FOUL-UPS... OLD FUELER'S LOADED FOR BEAR!
→HAR!← THERE WON'T BE NO FOUL-UPS!...
'CAUSE MY HOT DOG IS LOADED, TOO!
HERE, BOY!
WAKE UP, BOY... DAT'S IT... JUST LONG ENUFF TO CHOW DOWN!

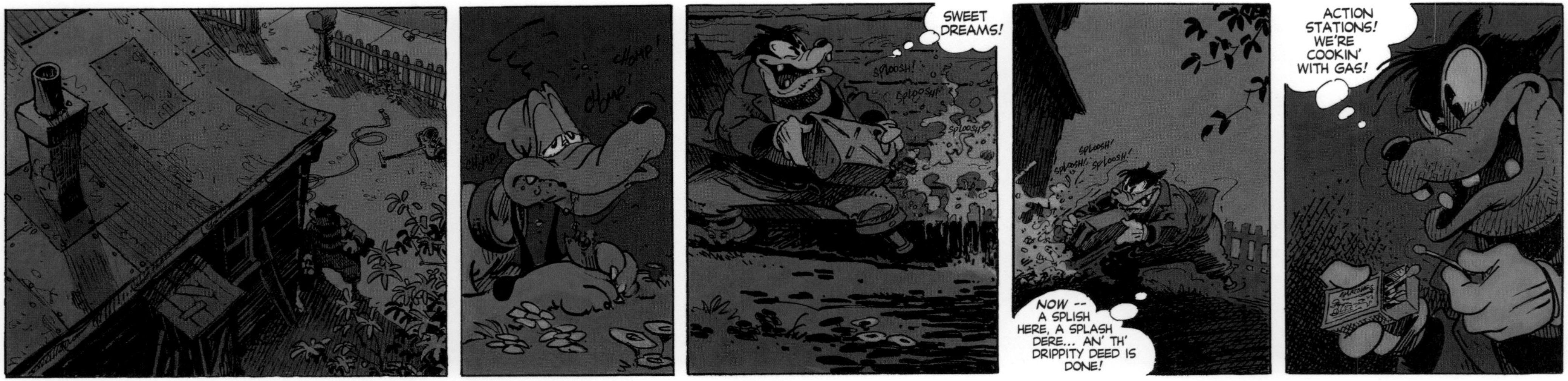

SWEET DREAMS!
NOW -- A SPLISH HERE, A SPLASH DERE... AN' TH' DRIPPITY DEED IS DONE!
ACTION STATIONS! WE'RE COOKIN' WITH GAS!

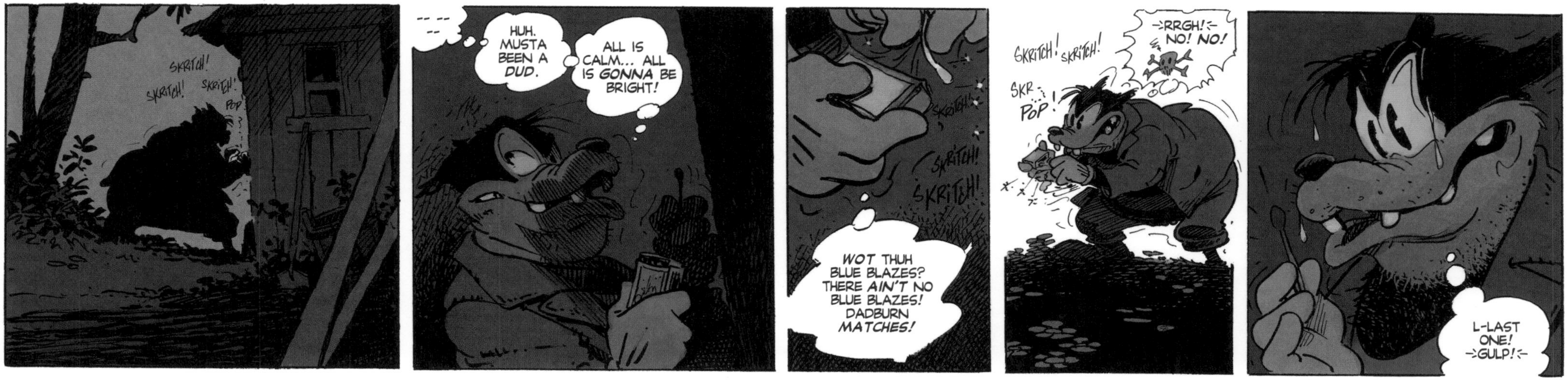
SKRITCH!
SKRITCH!
SKRITCH!
POP
HUH. MUSTA BEEN A *DUD*.
ALL IS CALM... ALL IS *GONNA* BE BRIGHT!
SKRITCH!
SKRITCH!
SKRITCH!
WOT THUH BLUE BLAZES? THERE *AIN'T* NO BLUE BLAZES! DADBURN *MATCHES!*
SKRITCH!
SKRITCH!
SKR... POP!
RRGH! NO! *NO!*
L-LAST ONE! GULP!

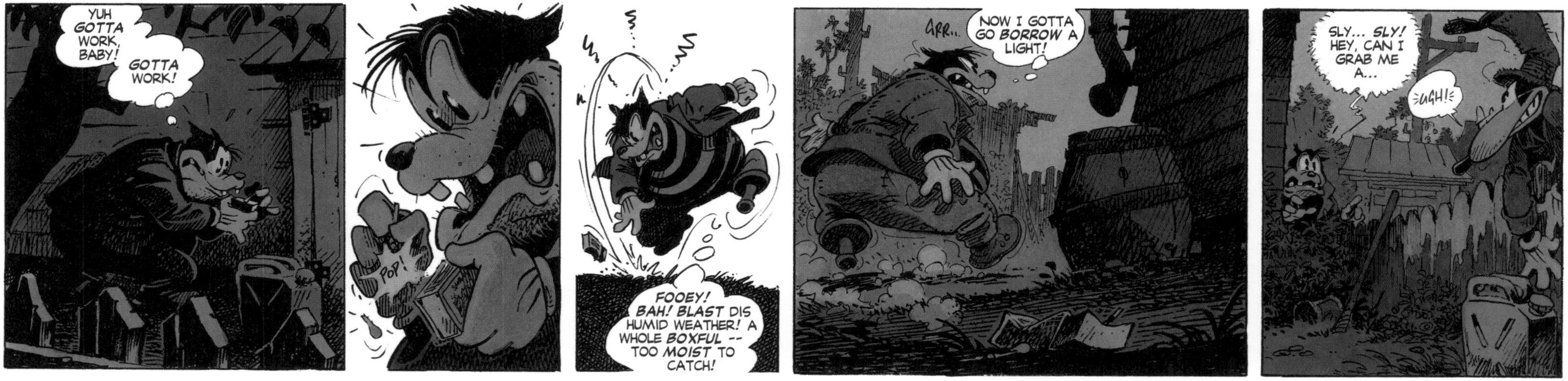
YUH *GOTTA* WORK, BABY!
GOTTA WORK!
POP!
FOOEY! BAH! BLAST DIS HUMID WEATHER! A WHOLE *BOXFUL* -- TOO *MOIST* TO CATCH!
GRR..
NOW I GOTTA GO *BORROW* A LIGHT!
SLY... *SLY!* HEY, CAN I GRAB ME A...
UGH!

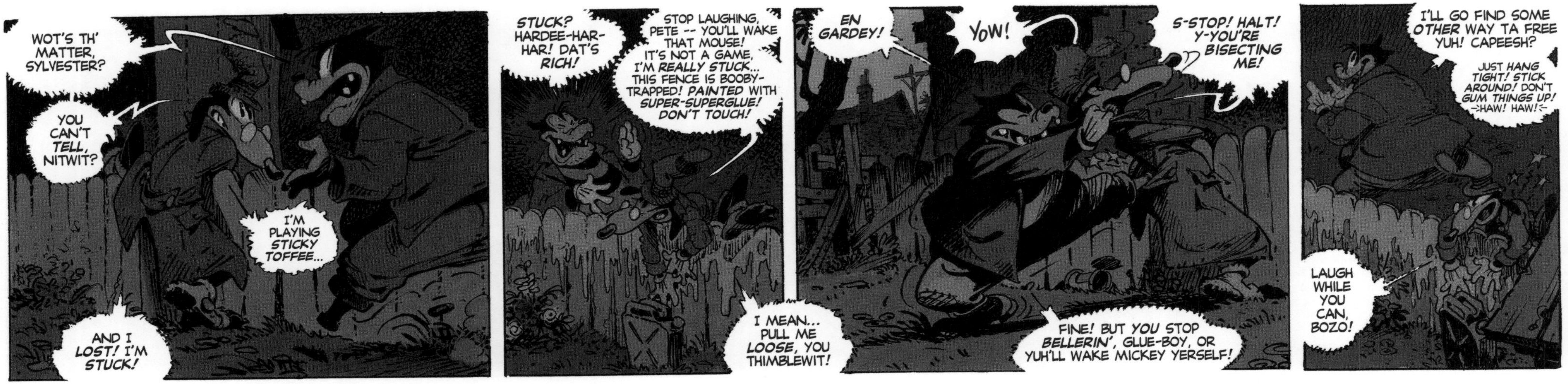
WOT'S TH' MATTER, SYLVESTER?
YOU CAN'T TELL, NITWIT?
I'M PLAYING STICKY TOFFEE...
AND I LOST! I'M STUCK!
STUCK? HARDEE-HAR-HAR! DAT'S RICH!
STOP LAUGHING, PETE -- YOU'LL WAKE THAT MOUSE! IT'S NOT A GAME, I'M REALLY STUCK... THIS FENCE IS BOOBY-TRAPPED! PAINTED WITH SUPER-SUPERGLUE! DON'T TOUCH!
I MEAN... PULL ME LOOSE, YOU THIMBLEWIT!
EN GARDEY!
YOW!
S-STOP! HALT! Y-YOU'RE BISECTING ME!
FINE! BUT YOU STOP BELLERIN', GLUE-BOY, OR YUH'LL WAKE MICKEY YERSELF!
I'LL GO FIND SOME OTHER WAY TA FREE YUH! CAPEESH?
JUST HANG TIGHT! STICK AROUND! DON'T GUM THINGS UP! -HAW! HAW!-
LAUGH WHILE YOU CAN, BOZO!

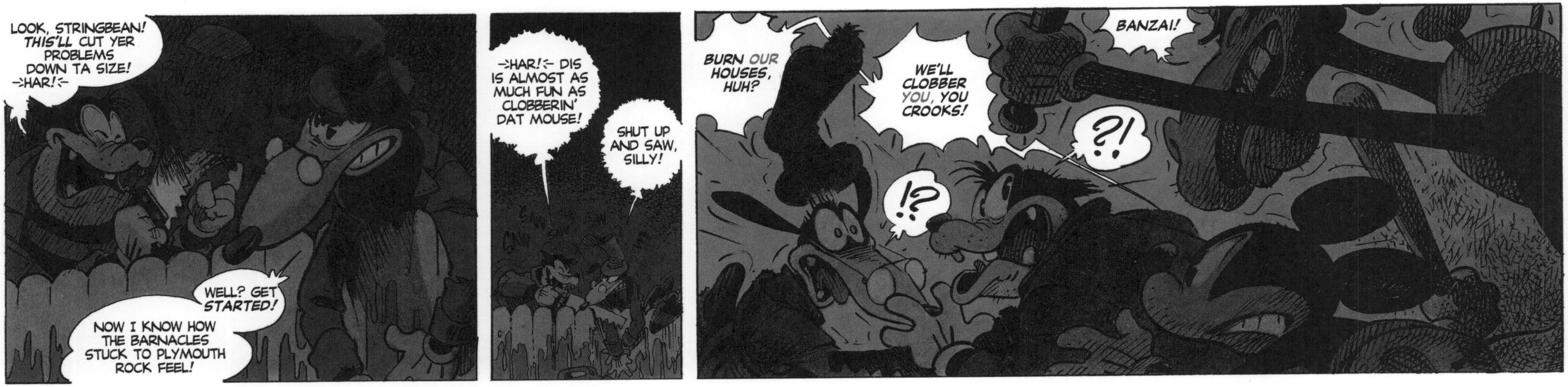
LOOK, STRINGBEAN! THIS'LL CUT YER PROBLEMS DOWN TA SIZE! -HAR!-
WELL? GET STARTED!
NOW I KNOW HOW THE BARNACLES STUCK TO PLYMOUTH ROCK FEEL!
-HAR!- DIS IS ALMOST AS MUCH FUN AS CLOBBERIN' DAT MOUSE!
SHUT UP AND SAW, SILLY!
BURN OUR HOUSES, HUH?
WE'LL CLOBBER YOU, YOU CROOKS!
BANZAI!
?!
!?

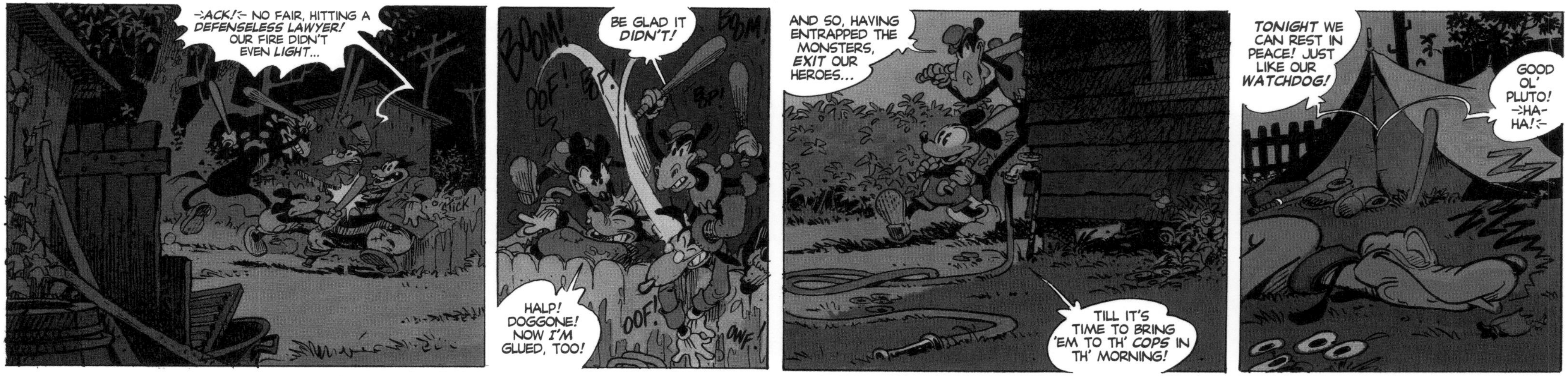
-ACK!- NO FAIR, HITTING A DEFENSELESS LAWYER! OUR FIRE DIDN'T EVEN LIGHT...
STICK!
BOOM!
OOF!
BE GLAD IT DIDN'T!
BOOM!
HALP! DOGGONE! NOW I'M GLUED, TOO!
OOF!
OWF!
AND SO, HAVING ENTRAPPED THE MONSTERS, EXIT OUR HEROES...
TILL IT'S TIME TO BRING 'EM TO TH' COPS IN TH' MORNING!
TONIGHT WE CAN REST IN PEACE! JUST LIKE OUR WATCHDOG!
GOOD OL' PLUTO! -HA-HA!-

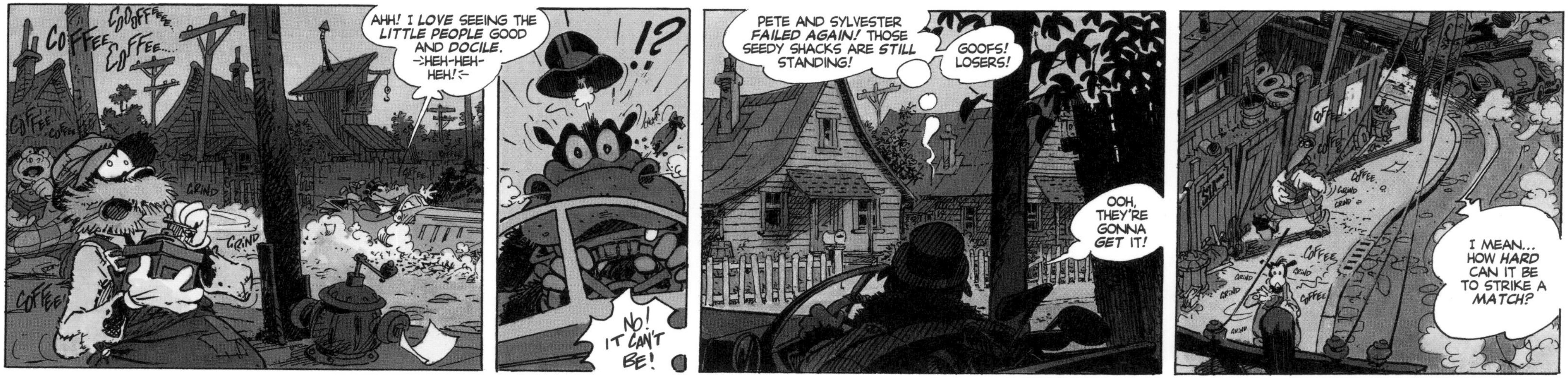
COFFEE COFFEE COFFEE... COOFFEE...
AHH! I LOVE SEEING THE LITTLE PEOPLE GOOD AND DOCILE. -HEH-HEH-HEH!-
GRIND
COFFEE!
!?
NO! IT CAN'T BE!
PETE AND SYLVESTER FAILED AGAIN! THOSE SEEDY SHACKS ARE STILL STANDING!
GOOFS! LOSERS!
OOH, THEY'RE GONNA GET IT!
COFFEE
GRIND
I MEAN... HOW HARD CAN IT BE TO STRIKE A MATCH?

-:EEP!:-

SCREEEEEEK

OKAY! I SEE NOW! I'M DEALING WITH DADBLASTED *BRAINS!* BUT THINGS MIGHT *NOT* KEEP GOING THEIR WAY!

IT'S UP TH' CREEK FOR YOU, BOYS!

YEAH!... -:TSK!:- ATTEMPTED ARSON! YOU'LL BE CHILLING THOSE HOT TEMPERS IN THE COOLER AWHILE!

BOPPITY-BOP! BOSS!

WHEEK! EEK!

THIS WAY, YOU CLOWNS!

GET UP AND GO!

VRRRBOOOO

VROOOO

40

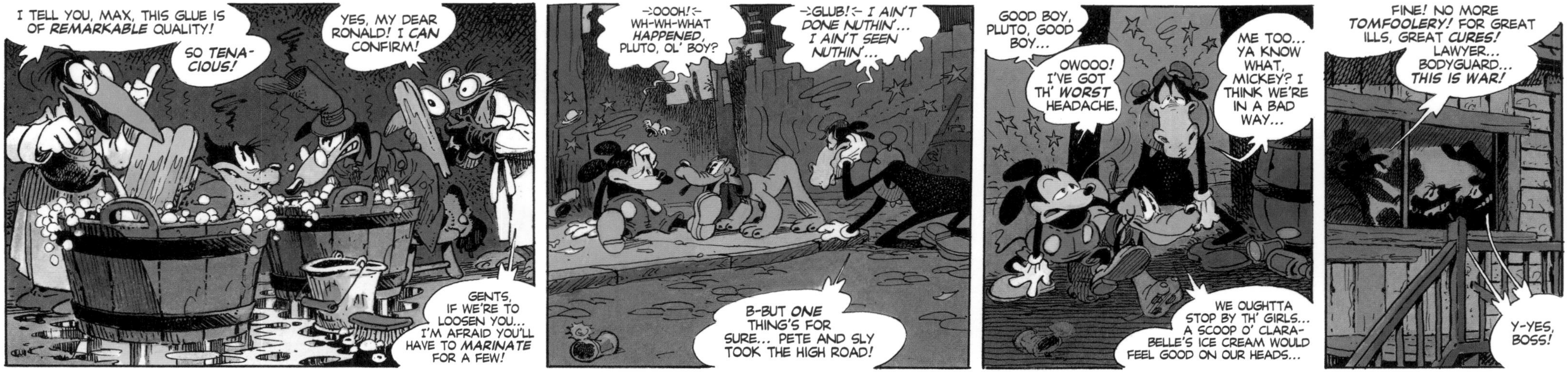
I TELL YOU, MAX, THIS GLUE IS OF *REMARKABLE* QUALITY!
SO *TENA-CIOUS!*
YES, MY DEAR RONALD! I *CAN* CONFIRM!
GENTS, IF WE'RE TO LOOSEN YOU... I'M AFRAID YOU'LL HAVE TO *MARINATE* FOR A FEW!
-OOOH!- WH-WH-WHAT *HAPPENED*, PLUTO, OL' BOY?
-GLUB!- *I AIN'T DONE NUTHIN'... I AIN'T SEEN NUTHIN'...*
B-BUT *ONE* THING'S FOR SURE... PETE AND SLY TOOK THE HIGH ROAD!
GOOD BOY, PLUTO, GOOD BOY...
OWOOO! I'VE GOT TH' *WORST* HEADACHE.
ME TOO... YA KNOW WHAT, MICKEY? I THINK WE'RE IN A BAD WAY...
WE OUGHTTA STOP BY TH' GIRLS... A SCOOP O' CLARA-BELLE'S ICE CREAM WOULD FEEL GOOD ON OUR HEADS...
FINE! NO MORE *TOMFOOLERY!* FOR GREAT ILLS, GREAT *CURES!* LAWYER... BODYGUARD... *THIS IS WAR!*
Y-YES, BOSS!

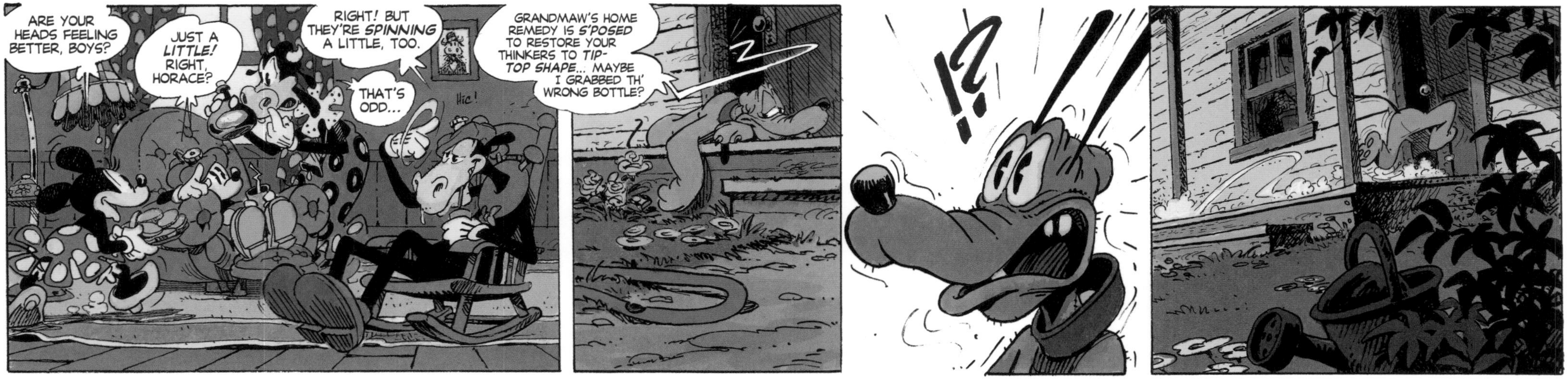
ARE YOUR HEADS FEELING BETTER, BOYS?
JUST A *LITTLE!* RIGHT, HORACE?
RIGHT! BUT THEY'RE *SPINNING* A LITTLE, TOO.
THAT'S ODD...
Hic!
GRANDMAW'S HOME REMEDY IS *S'POSED* TO RESTORE YOUR THINKERS TO *TIP-TOP SHAPE*... MAYBE I GRABBED TH' WRONG BOTTLE?
!?

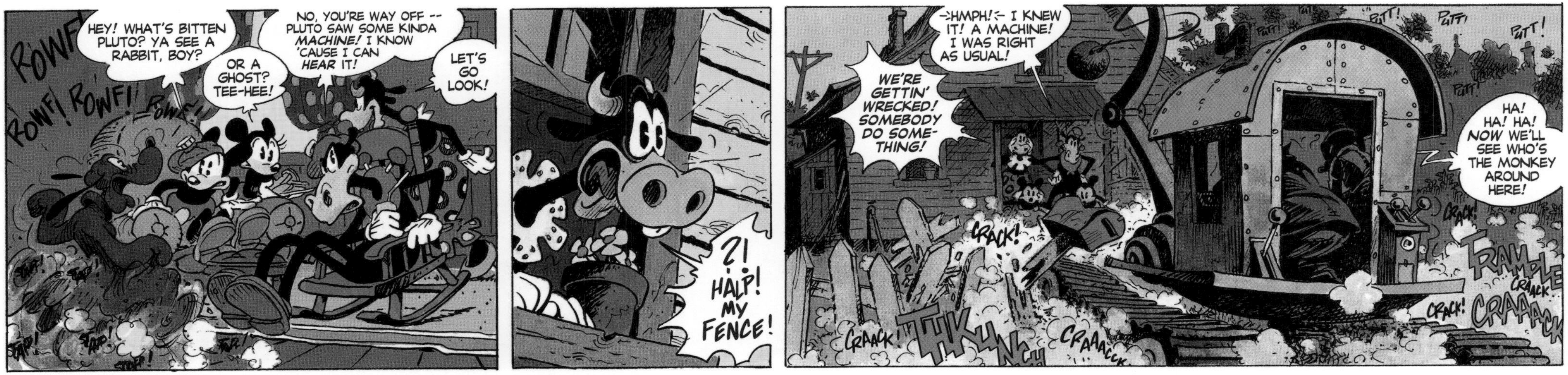
ROWF! ROWF! ROWF!
HEY! WHAT'S BITTEN PLUTO? YA SEE A RABBIT, BOY?
OR A GHOST? TEE-HEE!
NO, YOU'RE WAY OFF -- PLUTO SAW SOME KINDA *MACHINE!* I KNOW 'CAUSE I CAN *HEAR* IT!
LET'S GO LOOK!
?! HALP! MY FENCE!
WE'RE GETTIN' WRECKED! SOMEBODY DO SOME-THING!
-HMPH!- I KNEW IT! A MACHINE! I WAS RIGHT AS USUAL!
PUTT! PUTT! PUTT!
HA! HA! HA! *NOW* WE'LL SEE WHO'S THE MONKEY AROUND HERE!
CRACK! CRACK! CRACK!
TRAMPLE
CRAAACK
CRAACK!

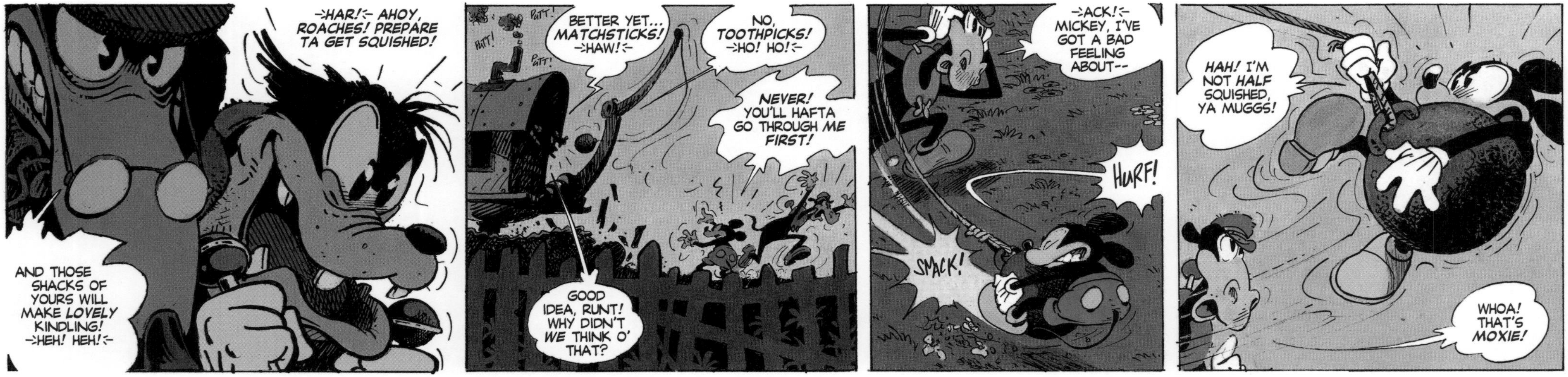
-HAR!- AHOY, ROACHES! PREPARE TA GET SQUISHED!
AND THOSE SHACKS OF YOURS WILL MAKE *LOVELY* KINDLING! -HEH! HEH!-
PUTT! PUTT! PUTT!
BETTER YET... *MATCHSTICKS!* -HAW!-
NO, *TOOTHPICKS!* -HO! HO!-
NEVER! YOU'LL HAFTA GO THROUGH ME *FIRST!*
GOOD IDEA, RUNT! WHY DIDN'T *WE* THINK O' THAT?
-ACK!- MICKEY, I'VE GOT A BAD FEELING ABOUT--
HURF!
SMACK!
HAH! I'M NOT *HALF* SQUISHED, YA MUGGS!
WHOA! THAT'S *MOXIE!*

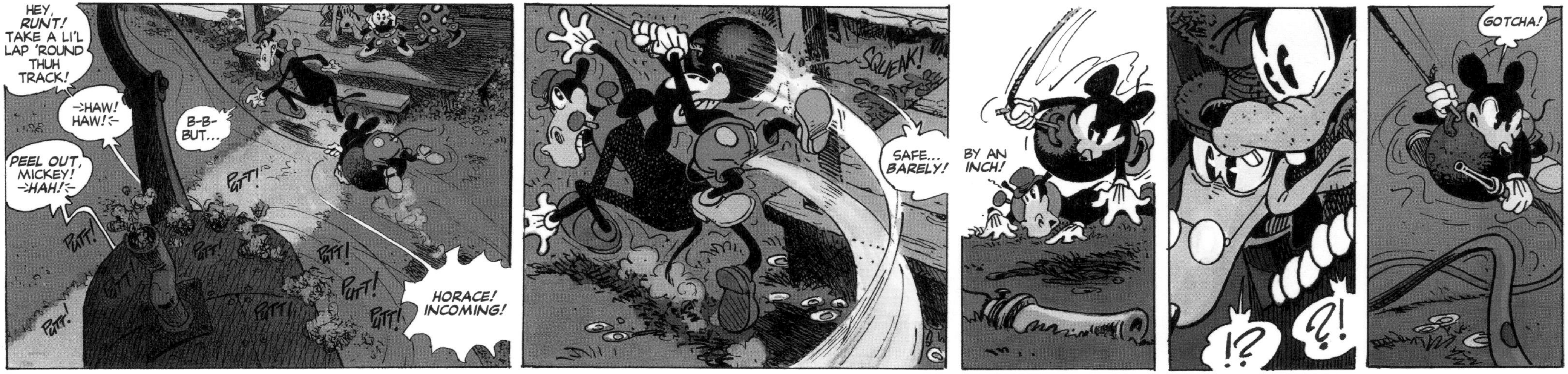
HEY, RUNT! TAKE A LI'L LAP 'ROUND THUH TRACK!
HAW! HAW!
PEEL OUT, MICKEY! HAH!
B-B-BUT...
PUTT!
PUTT!
PUTT!
PUTT!
PUTT!
PUTT!
PUTT!
PUTT!
HORACE! INCOMING!
SQUEAK!
SAFE... BARELY!
BY AN INCH!
!?
?!
GOTCHA!

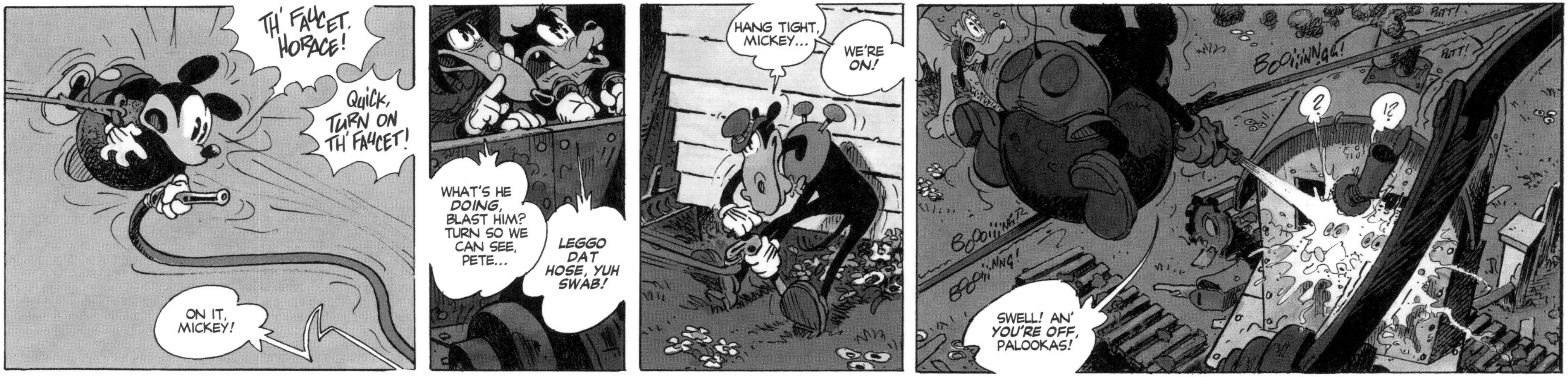
TH' FAUCET, HORACE!
QUICK, TURN ON TH' FAUCET!
ON IT, MICKEY!
WHAT'S HE DOING, BLAST HIM? TURN SO WE CAN SEE, PETE...
LEGGO DAT HOSE, YUH SWAB!
HANG TIGHT, MICKEY...
WE'RE ON!
BOOIIINNGG!
PUTT!
PUTT!
?
!?
BOOIIINNGG!
BOOIIINNG!
SWELL! AN' YOU'RE OFF, PALOOKAS!

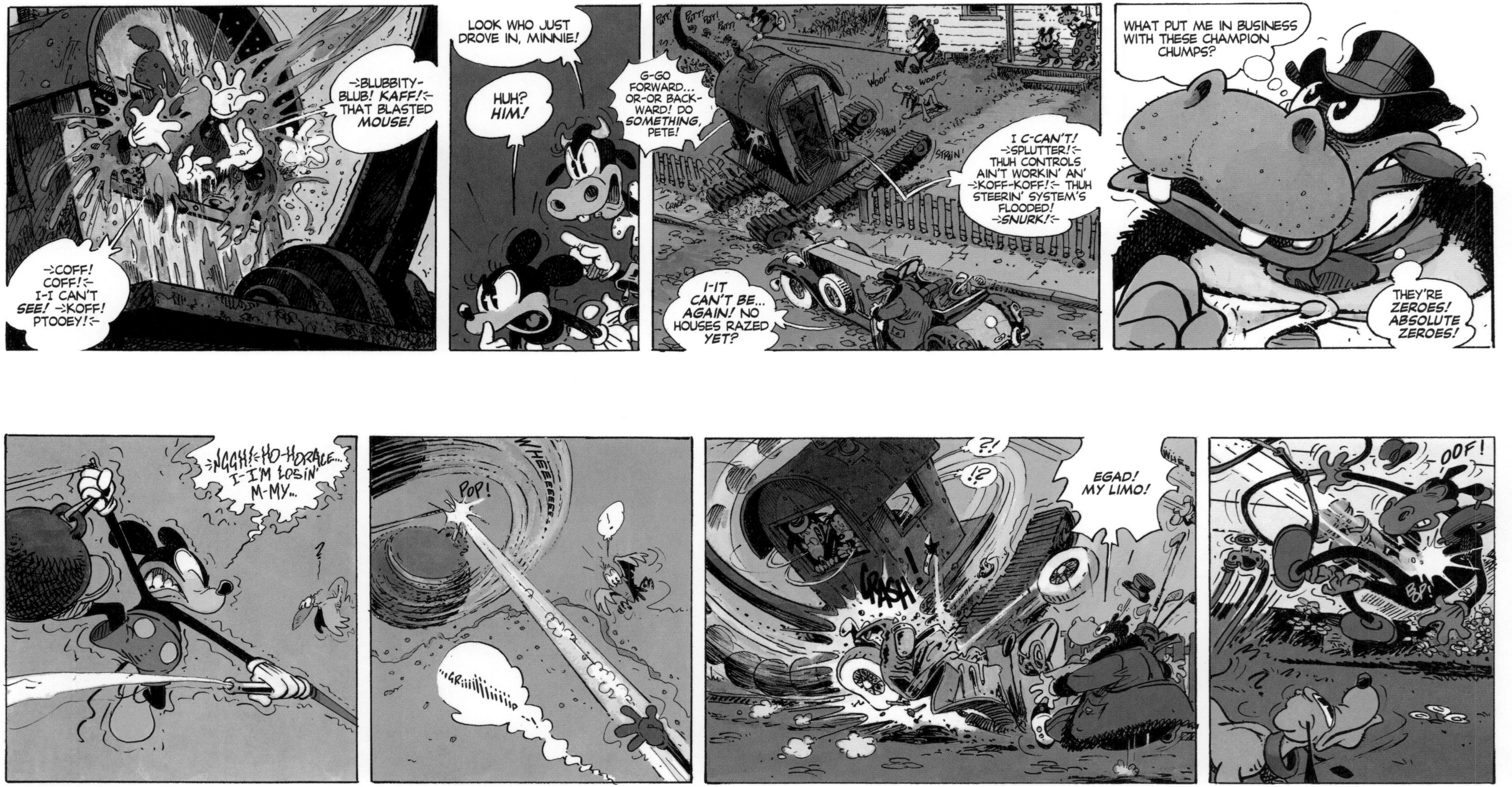
–BLUBBITY-BLUB! KAFF!– THAT BLASTED MOUSE!
–COFF! COFF!– I-I CAN'T SEE! –KOFF! PTOOEY!–
LOOK WHO JUST DROVE IN, MINNIE!
HUH? HIM!
PUTT! PUTT! PUTT!
G-GO FORWARD... OR-OR BACKWARD! DO SOMETHING, PETE!
WOOF! WOOF!
STRAIN STRAIN!
I C-CAN'T! –SPLUTTER!– THUH CONTROLS AIN'T WORKIN' AN' –KOFF-KOFF!– THUH STEERIN' SYSTEM'S FLOODED! –SNURK!–
I-IT CAN'T BE... AGAIN! NO HOUSES RAZED YET?
WHAT PUT ME IN BUSINESS WITH THESE CHAMPION CHUMPS?
THEY'RE ZEROES! ABSOLUTE ZEROES!
–NGGH!– HO-HORACE... I-I'M LOSIN' M-MY...
?
WHEEEEEEE
POP!
!
?!
!?
EGAD! MY LIMO!
CRASH!
OOF!
BOP!
?

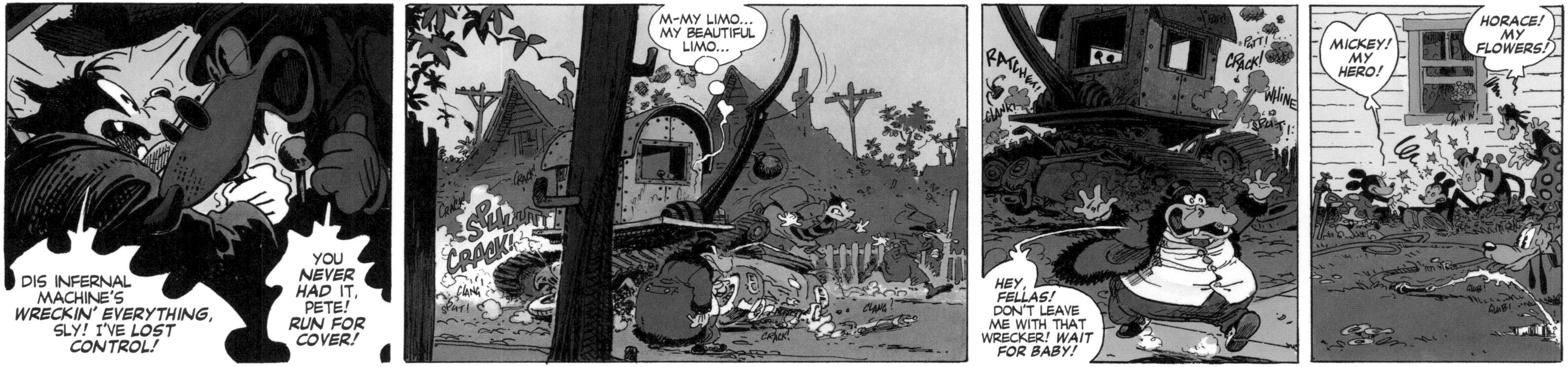
DIS INFERNAL MACHINE'S WRECKIN' EVERYTHING, SLY! I'VE LOST CONTROL!
YOU NEVER HAD IT, PETE! RUN FOR COVER!
M-MY LIMO... MY BEAUTIFUL LIMO...
SPLUTT
CRACK!
CRACK!
HEY, FELLAS! DON'T LEAVE ME WITH THAT WRECKER! WAIT FOR BABY!
CRACK!
WHINE
MICKEY! MY HERO!
HORACE! MY FLOWERS!

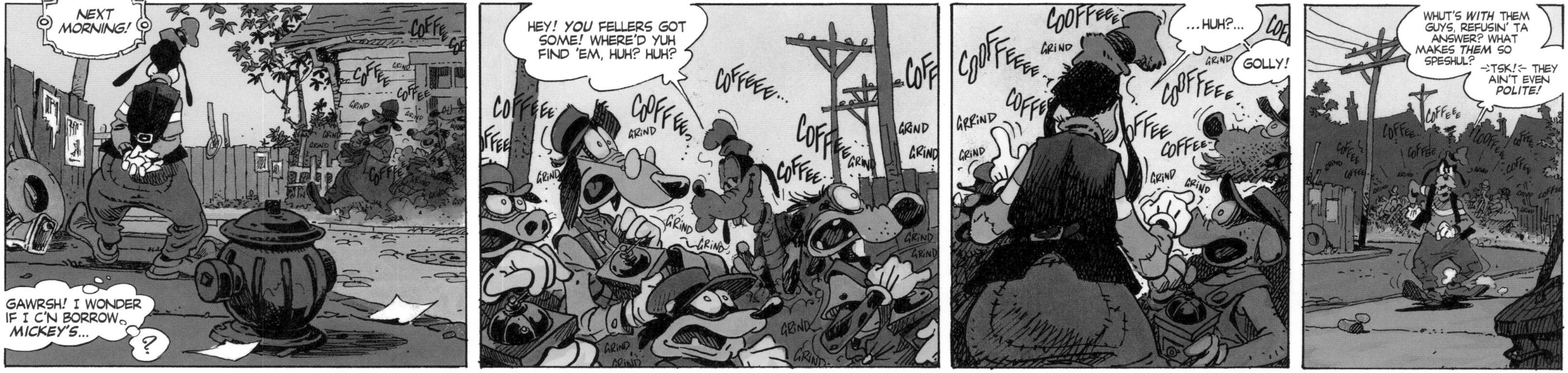
NEXT MORNING!
GAWRSH! I WONDER IF I C'N BORROW MICKEY'S...
?
HEY! YOU FELLERS GOT SOME! WHERE'D YUH FIND 'EM, HUH? HUH?
COFFEEE...
COFFEE
GRIND
...HUH?...
GOLLY!
COOFFEEE
WHUT'S WITH THEM GUYS, REFUSIN' TA ANSWER? WHAT MAKES THEM SO SPESHUL?
TSK! THEY AIN'T EVEN POLITE!

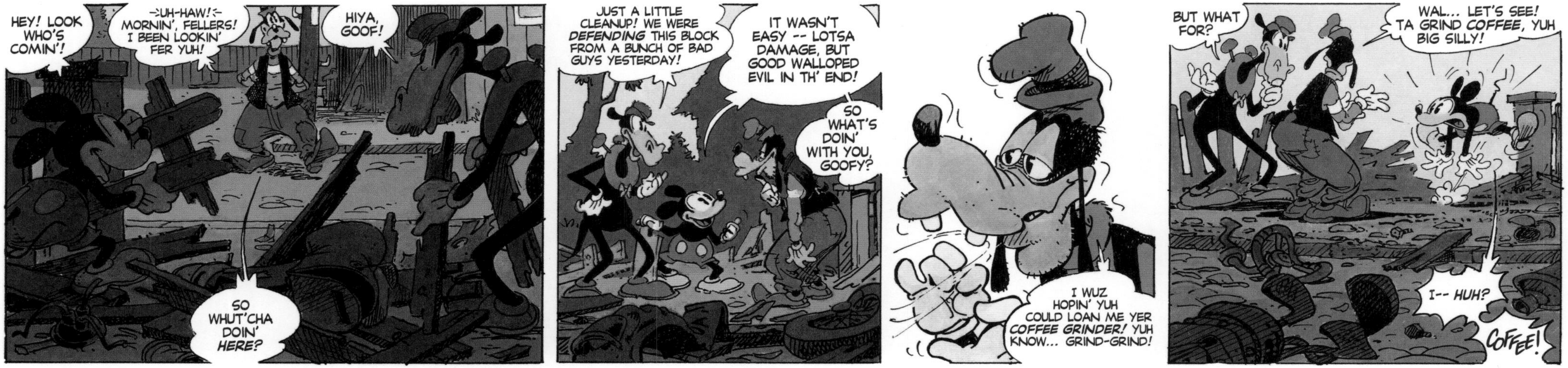
HEY! LOOK WHO'S COMIN'!
-›UH-HAW!‹- MORNIN', FELLERS! I BEEN LOOKIN' FER YUH!
HIYA, GOOF!
SO WHUT'CHA DOIN' HERE?
JUST A LITTLE CLEANUP! WE WERE DEFENDING THIS BLOCK FROM A BUNCH OF BAD GUYS YESTERDAY!
IT WASN'T EASY -- LOTSA DAMAGE, BUT GOOD WALLOPED EVIL IN TH' END!
SO WHAT'S DOIN' WITH YOU, GOOFY?
I WUZ HOPIN' YUH COULD LOAN ME YER COFFEE GRINDER! YUH KNOW... GRIND-GRIND!
BUT WHAT FOR?
WAL... LET'S SEE! TA GRIND COFFEE, YUH BIG SILLY!
I-- HUH?
COFFEE!

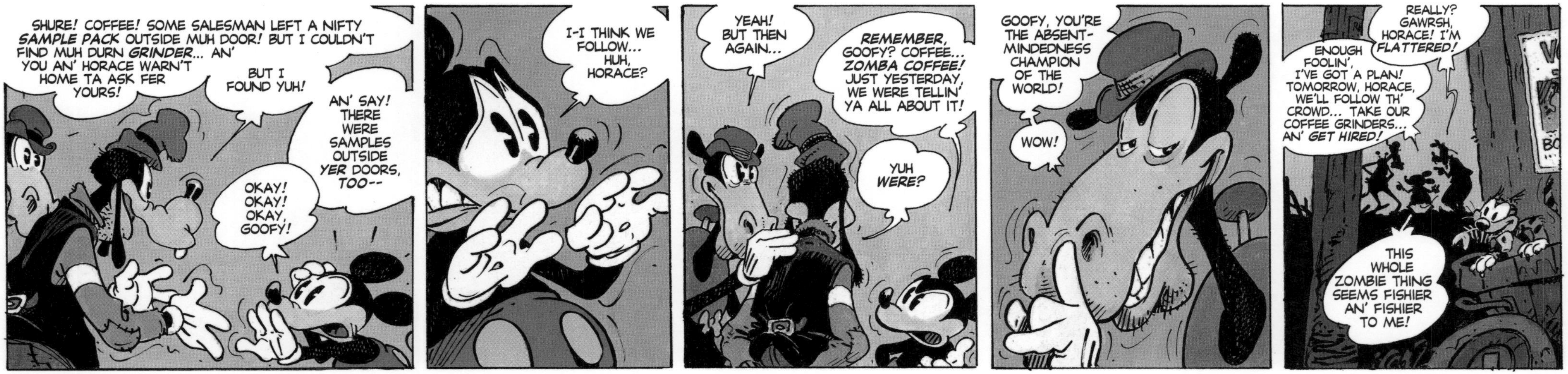
SHURE! COFFEE! SOME SALESMAN LEFT A NIFTY SAMPLE PACK OUTSIDE MUH DOOR! BUT I COULDN'T FIND MUH DURN GRINDER... AN' YOU AN' HORACE WARN'T HOME TA ASK FER YOURS!
BUT I FOUND YUH!
AN' SAY! THERE WERE SAMPLES OUTSIDE YER DOORS, TOO--
OKAY! OKAY! OKAY, GOOFY!
I-I THINK WE FOLLOW... HUH, HORACE?
YEAH! BUT THEN AGAIN...
REMEMBER, GOOFY? COFFEE... ZOMBA COFFEE! JUST YESTERDAY, WE WERE TELLIN' YA ALL ABOUT IT!
YUH WERE?
GOOFY, YOU'RE THE ABSENT-MINDEDNESS CHAMPION OF THE WORLD!
WOW!
REALLY? GAWRSH, HORACE! I'M FLATTERED!
ENOUGH FOOLIN', I'VE GOT A PLAN! TOMORROW, HORACE, WE'LL FOLLOW TH' CROWD... TAKE OUR COFFEE GRINDERS... AN' GET HIRED!
THIS WHOLE ZOMBIE THING SEEMS FISHIER AN' FISHIER TO ME!

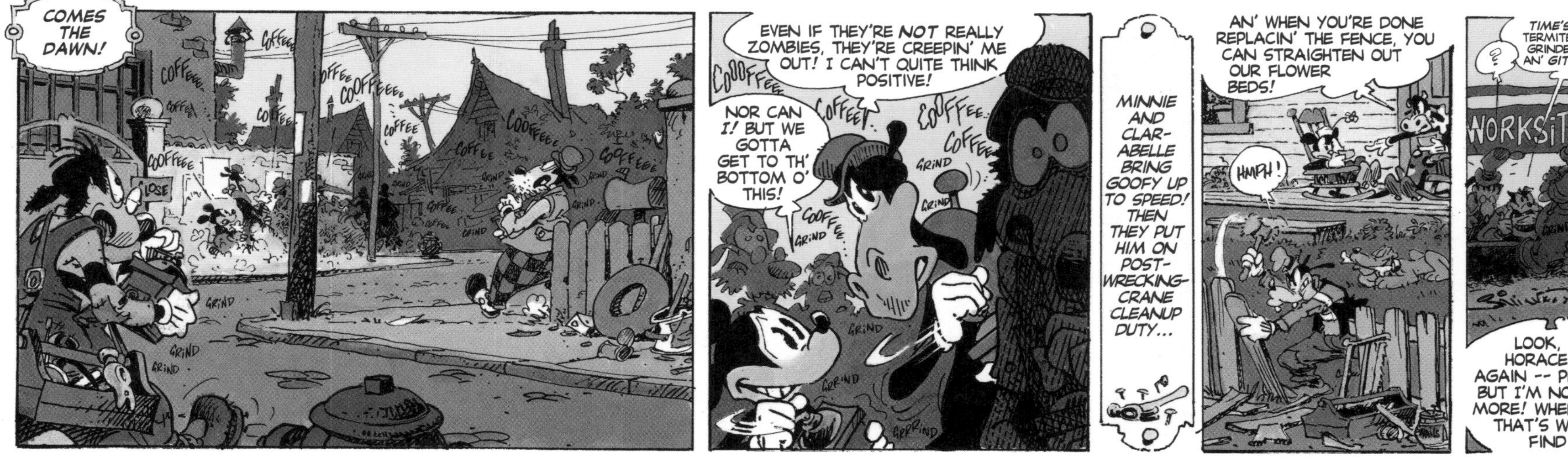
COMES THE DAWN!
LOSE
EVEN IF THEY'RE NOT REALLY ZOMBIES, THEY'RE CREEPIN' ME OUT! I CAN'T QUITE THINK POSITIVE!
NOR CAN I! BUT WE GOTTA GET TO TH' BOTTOM O' THIS!
MINNIE AND CLARABELLE BRING GOOFY UP TO SPEED! THEN THEY PUT HIM ON POST-WRECKING-CRANE CLEANUP DUTY...
AN' WHEN YOU'RE DONE REPLACIN' THE FENCE, YOU CAN STRAIGHTEN OUT OUR FLOWER BEDS!
HMPH!
TIME'S A-WASTIN', YOU TERMITES! DROP YER COFFEE GRINDERS, GRAB YER TOOLS AN' GIT TA WORK!
WORKSITE
LOOK, HORACE, IT'S THEM AGAIN -- PETE AN' SYLVESTER! BUT I'M NOT SURPRISED ANYMORE! WHERE THERE'S TROUBLE, THAT'S WHERE YOU'LL FIND THEM!
GRR! JUST YOU WAIT!

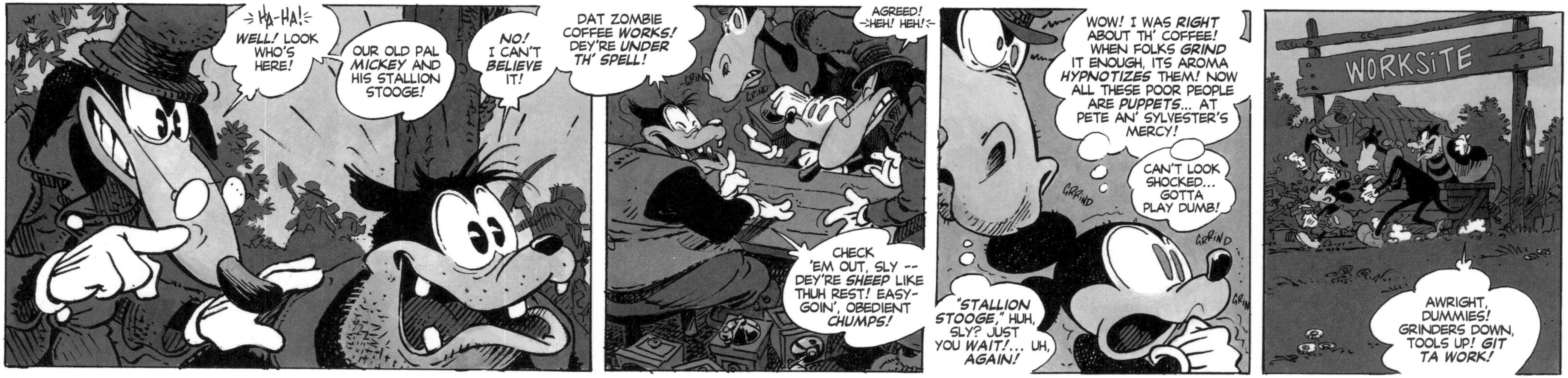
HA-HA!
WELL! LOOK WHO'S HERE!
OUR OLD PAL MICKEY AND HIS STALLION STOOGE!
NO! I CAN'T BELIEVE IT!
DAT ZOMBIE COFFEE WORKS! DEY'RE UNDER TH' SPELL!
AGREED! HEH! HEH!
CHECK 'EM OUT, SLY -- DEY'RE SHEEP LIKE THUH REST! EASY-GOIN', OBEDIENT CHUMPS!
WOW! I WAS RIGHT ABOUT TH' COFFEE! WHEN FOLKS GRIND IT ENOUGH, ITS AROMA HYPNOTIZES THEM! NOW ALL THESE POOR PEOPLE ARE PUPPETS... AT PETE AN' SYLVESTER'S MERCY!
CAN'T LOOK SHOCKED... GOTTA PLAY DUMB!
"STALLION STOOGE," HUH, SLY? JUST YOU WAIT!... UH, AGAIN!
WORKSITE
AWRIGHT, DUMMIES! GRINDERS DOWN, TOOLS UP! GIT TA WORK!

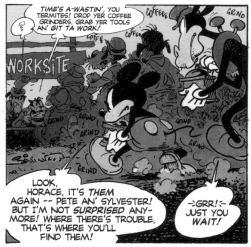

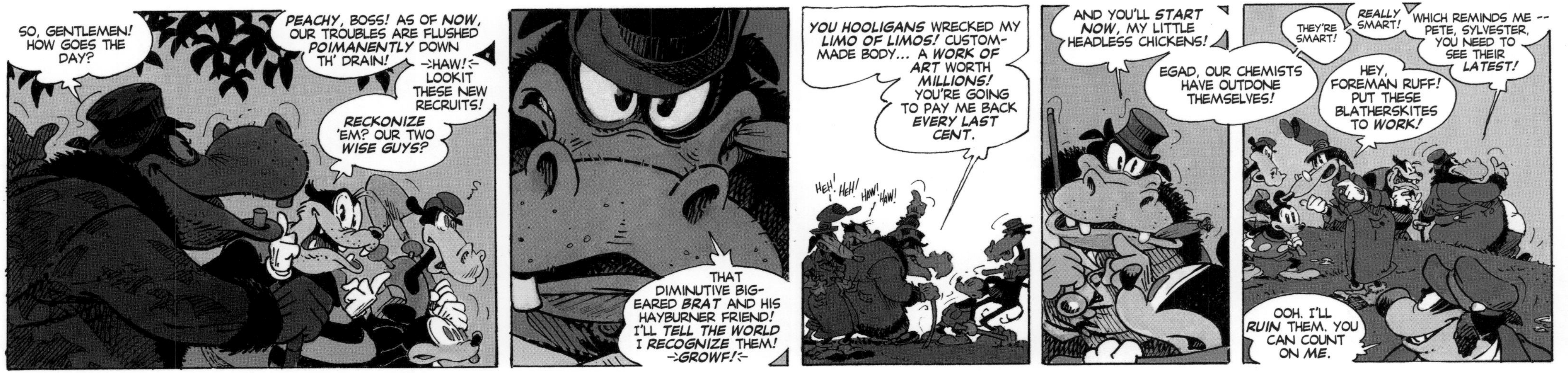
SO, GENTLEMEN! HOW GOES THE DAY?
PEACHY, BOSS! AS OF NOW, OUR TROUBLES ARE FLUSHED POIMANENTLY DOWN TH' DRAIN!
-HAW!- LOOKIT THESE NEW RECRUITS!
RECKONIZE 'EM? OUR TWO WISE GUYS?
THAT DIMINUTIVE BIG-EARED BRAT AND HIS HAYBURNER FRIEND! I'LL TELL THE WORLD I RECOGNIZE THEM! -GROWF!-
YOU HOOLIGANS WRECKED MY LIMO OF LIMOS! CUSTOM-MADE BODY... A WORK OF ART WORTH MILLIONS! YOU'RE GOING TO PAY ME BACK EVERY LAST CENT.
HEH! HEH! HAW! HAW!
AND YOU'LL START NOW, MY LITTLE HEADLESS CHICKENS!
EGAD, OUR CHEMISTS HAVE OUTDONE THEMSELVES!
THEY'RE SMART!
REALLY SMART!
WHICH REMINDS ME -- PETE, SYLVESTER, YOU NEED TO SEE THEIR LATEST!
HEY, FOREMAN RUFF! PUT THESE BLATHERSKITES TO WORK!
OOH. I'LL RUIN THEM. YOU CAN COUNT ON ME.

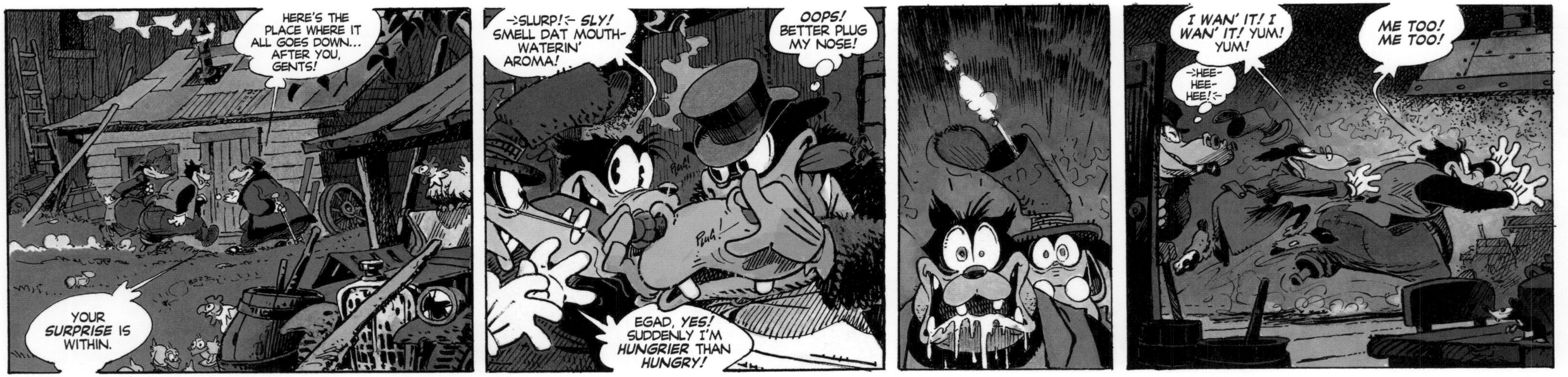
HERE'S THE PLACE WHERE IT ALL GOES DOWN... AFTER YOU, GENTS!
YOUR SURPRISE IS WITHIN.
-SLURP!- SLY! SMELL DAT MOUTH-WATERIN' AROMA!
OOPS! BETTER PLUG MY NOSE!
PLUG!
EGAD, YES! SUDDENLY I'M HUNGRIER THAN HUNGRY!
I WAN' IT! I WAN' IT! YUM! YUM!
-HEE-HEE-HEE!-
ME TOO! ME TOO!

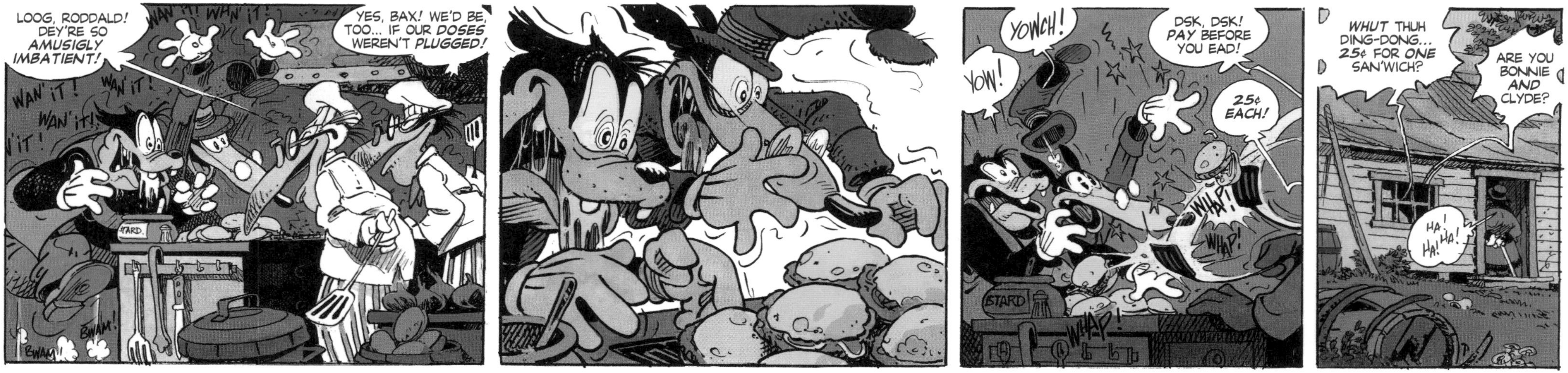
WAN' IT! WAN' IT!
LOOG, RODDALD! DEY'RE SO AMUSIGLY IMBATIENT!
YES, BAX! WE'D BE, TOO... IF OUR DOSES WEREN'T PLUGGED!
WAN' IT! WAN' IT! WAN' IT! WAN' IT!
STARD.
BWAM! BWAM!
YOWCH!
YOW!
DSK, DSK! PAY BEFORE YOU EAD!
25¢ EACH!
WHAP! WHAP! WHAP!
STARD
WHUT THUH DING-DONG... 25¢ FOR ONE SAN'WICH?
ARE YOU BONNIE AND CLYDE?
HA! HA! HA!

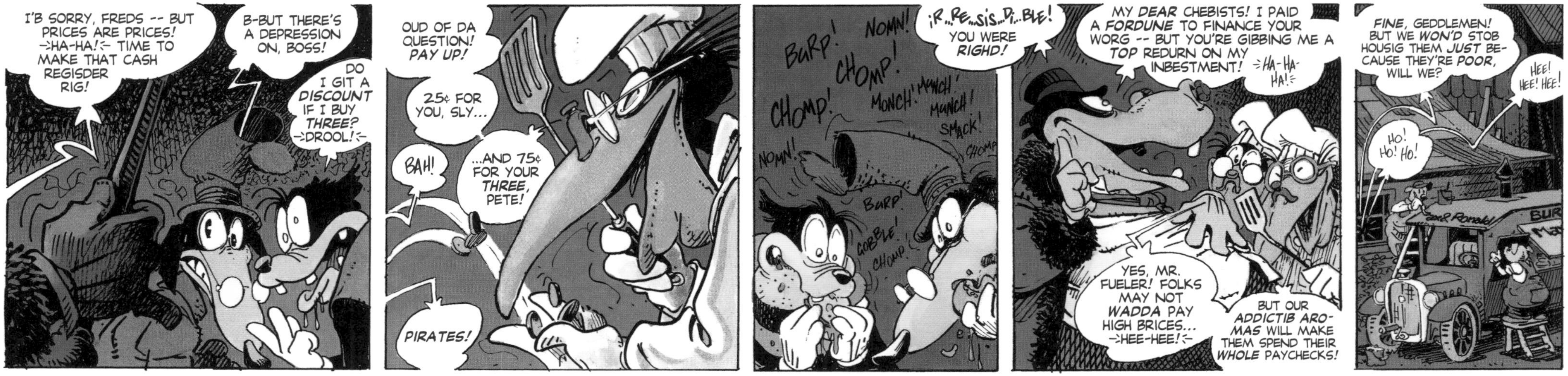
I'B SORRY, FREDS -- BUT PRICES ARE PRICES! -HA-HA!- TIME TO MAKE THAT CASH REGISDER RIG!
B-BUT THERE'S A DEPRESSION ON, BOSS!
DO I GIT A DISCOUNT IF I BUY THREE? -DROOL!-
OUD OF DA QUESTION! PAY UP!
25¢ FOR YOU, SLY...
...AND 75¢ FOR YOUR THREE, PETE!
BAH!
PIRATES!
BURP! CHOMP! NOMN! CHOMP! MONCH! MUNCH! MUNCH! SMACK! CHOMP NOMN!
BURP! GOBBLE! CHOMP!
¡R..RE..SIS..DI..BLE! YOU WERE RIGHD!
MY DEAR CHEBISTS! I PAID A FORDUNE TO FINANCE YOUR WORG -- BUT YOU'RE GIBBING ME A TOP REDURN ON MY INBESTMENT! -HA-HA-HA!-
YES, MR. FUELER! FOLKS MAY NOT WADDA PAY HIGH BRICES... -HEE-HEE!-
BUT OUR ADDICTIB AROMAS WILL MAKE THEM SPEND THEIR WHOLE PAYCHECKS!
FINE, GEDDLEMEN! BUT WE WON'D STOB HOUSIG THEM JUST BECAUSE THEY'RE POOR, WILL WE?
HEE! HEE! HEE!
HO! HO! HO!

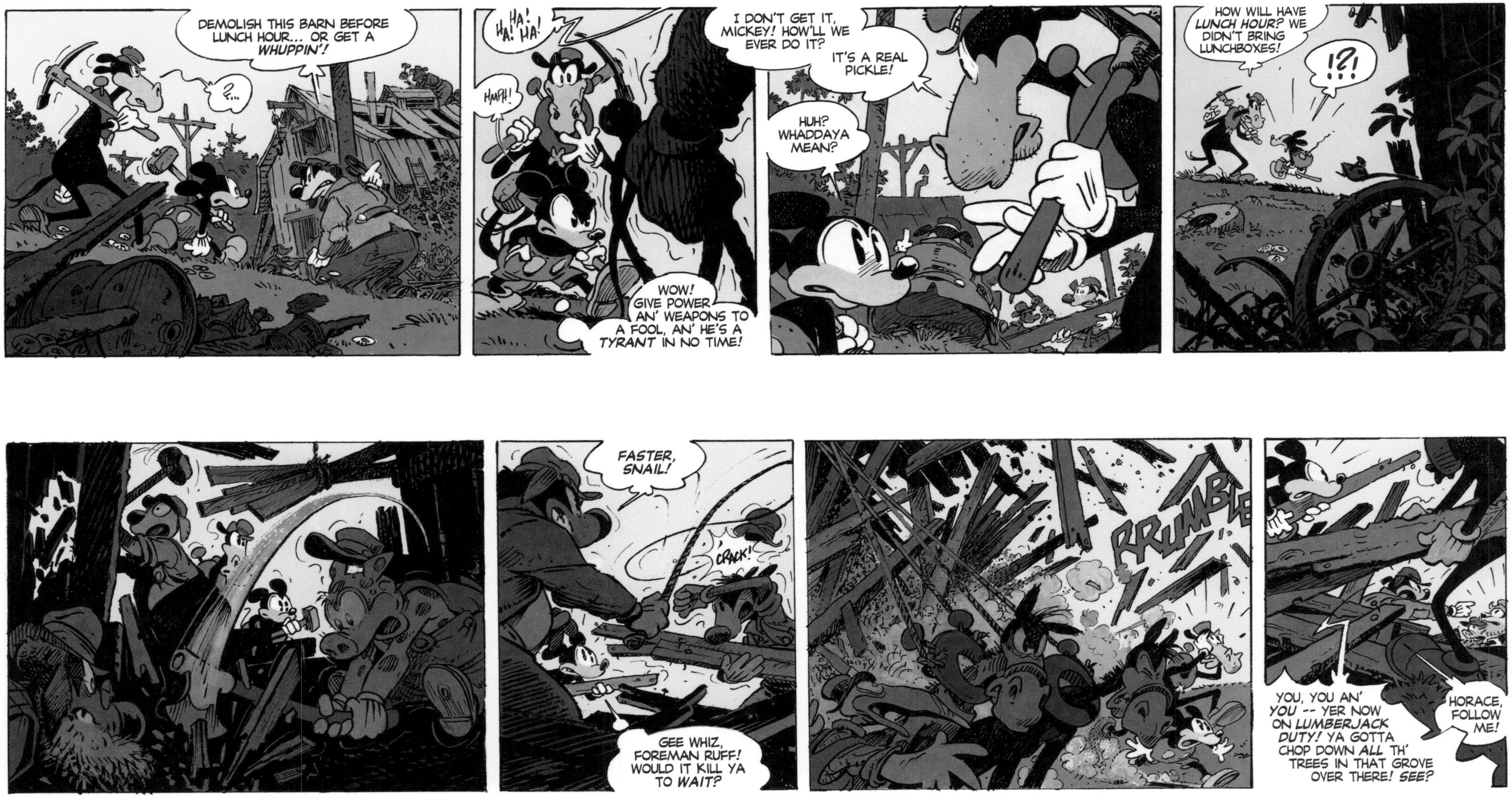
DEMOLISH THIS BARN BEFORE LUNCH HOUR... OR GET A WHUPPIN'!
?...
HA! HA! HA!
HMPH!
WOW! GIVE POWER AN' WEAPONS TO A FOOL, AN' HE'S A TYRANT IN NO TIME!
I DON'T GET IT, MICKEY! HOW'LL WE EVER DO IT?
IT'S A REAL PICKLE!
HUH? WHADDAYA MEAN?
HOW WILL HAVE LUNCH HOUR? WE DIDN'T BRING LUNCHBOXES!
!?!
FASTER, SNAIL!
CRACK!
GEE WHIZ, FOREMAN RUFF! WOULD IT KILL YA TO WAIT?
RRUMBLE
YOU, YOU AN' YOU -- YER NOW ON LUMBERJACK DUTY! YA GOTTA CHOP DOWN ALL TH' TREES IN THAT GROVE OVER THERE! SEE?
HORACE, FOLLOW ME!

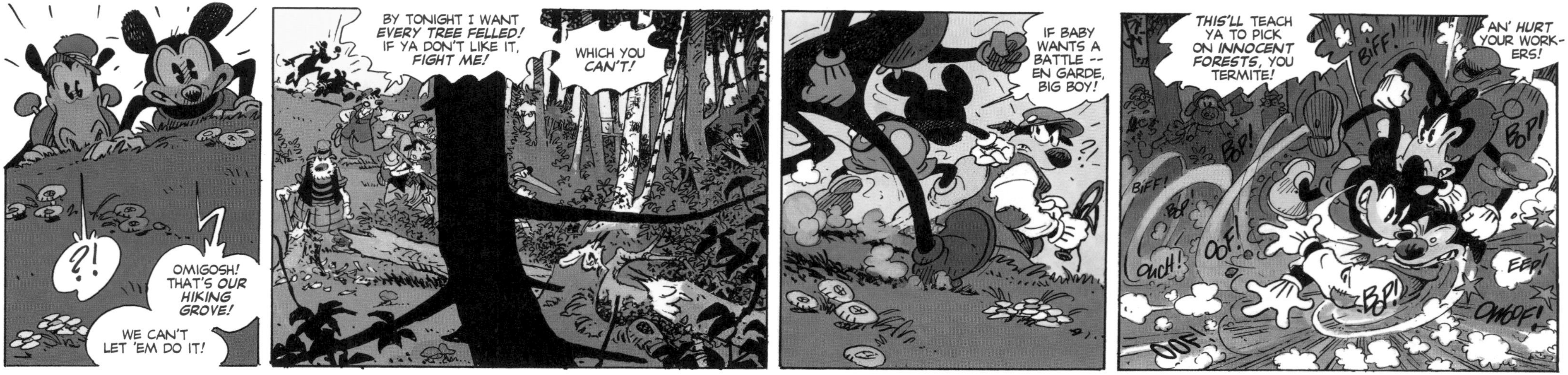
?!
OMIGOSH! THAT'S OUR HIKING GROVE!
WE CAN'T LET 'EM DO IT!
BY TONIGHT I WANT EVERY TREE FELLED! IF YA DON'T LIKE IT, FIGHT ME!
WHICH YOU CAN'T!
IF BABY WANTS A BATTLE -- EN GARDE, BIG BOY!
THIS'LL TEACH YA TO PICK ON INNOCENT FORESTS, YOU TERMITE!
AN' HURT YOUR WORKERS!
BIFF!
BOP!
BIFF!
BOP!
OUCH!
OOF!
BOP!
EEP!
OWOOF!
OOF

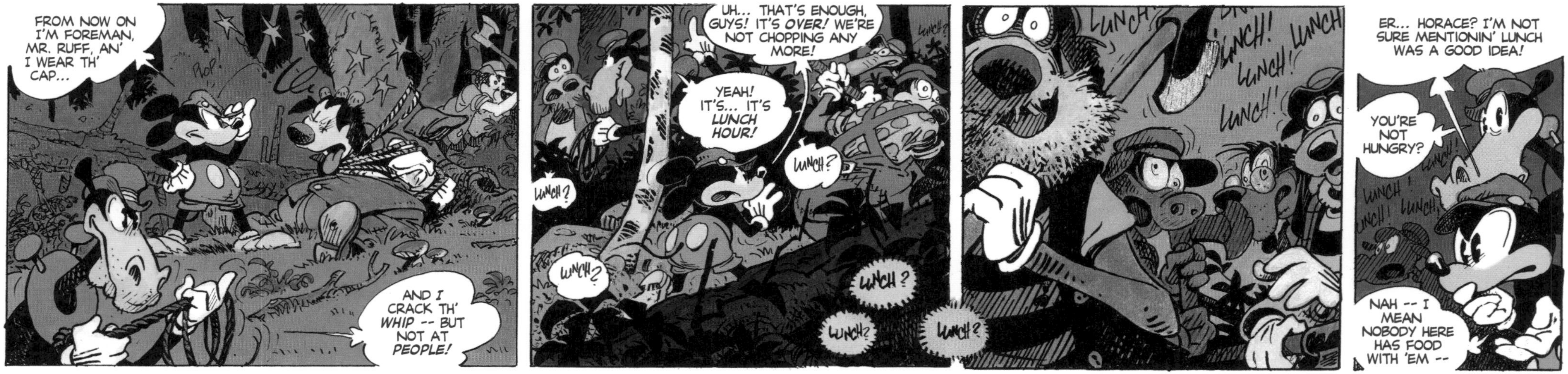
FROM NOW ON I'M FOREMAN, MR. RUFF, AN' I WEAR TH' CAP...
POP
AND I CRACK TH' WHIP -- BUT NOT AT PEOPLE!
UH... THAT'S ENOUGH, GUYS! IT'S OVER! WE'RE NOT CHOPPING ANY MORE!
YEAH! IT'S... IT'S LUNCH HOUR!
LUNCH?
LUNCH?
LUNCH?
LUNCH?
LUNCH?
LUNCH?
LUNCH!
LUNCH!
LUNCH!
LUNCH!
ER... HORACE? I'M NOT SURE MENTIONIN' LUNCH WAS A GOOD IDEA!
YOU'RE NOT HUNGRY?
LUNCH!
LUNCH!
LUNCH!
NAH -- I MEAN NOBODY HERE HAS FOOD WITH 'EM --

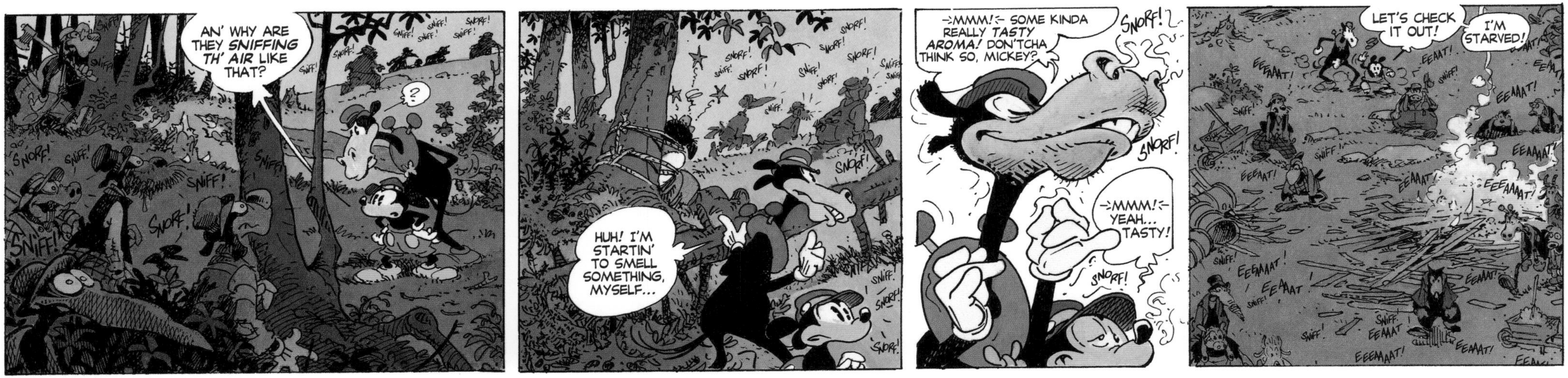
AN' WHY ARE THEY SNIFFING TH' AIR LIKE THAT?
?
SNIFF!
SNORF!
HUH! I'M STARTIN' TO SMELL SOMETHING, MYSELF...
SNORF!
→MMM!← SOME KINDA REALLY TASTY AROMA! DON'TCHA THINK SO, MICKEY?
SNORF!
→MMM!← YEAH... TASTY!
SNORF!
LET'S CHECK IT OUT!
I'M STARVED!
EEEAAAT!

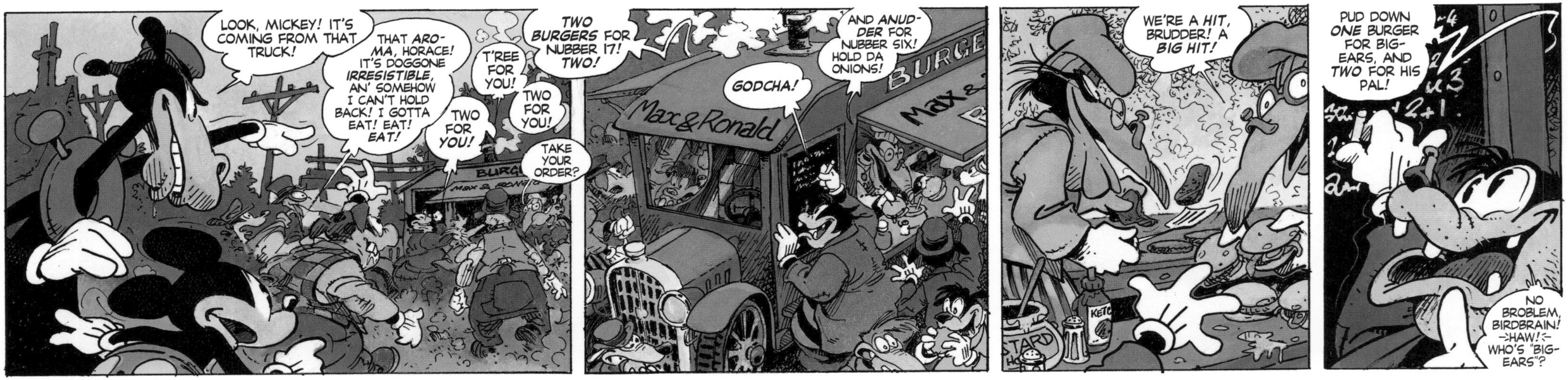
LOOK, MICKEY! IT'S COMING FROM THAT TRUCK!
THAT AROMA, HORACE! IT'S DOGGONE IRRESISTIBLE, AN' SOMEHOW I CAN'T HOLD BACK! I GOTTA EAT! EAT! EAT!
TWO FOR YOU!
T'REE FOR YOU!
TWO FOR YOU!
TAKE YOUR ORDER?
TWO BURGERS FOR NUBBER 17! TWO!
AND ANUDDER FOR NUBBER SIX! HOLD DA ONIONS!
GODCHA!
Max & Ronald
WE'RE A HIT, BRUDDER! A BIG HIT!
PUD DOWN ONE BURGER FOR BIG-EARS, AND TWO FOR HIS PAL!
NO BROBLEM, BIRDBRAIN! →HAW!← WHO'S "BIG-EARS"?

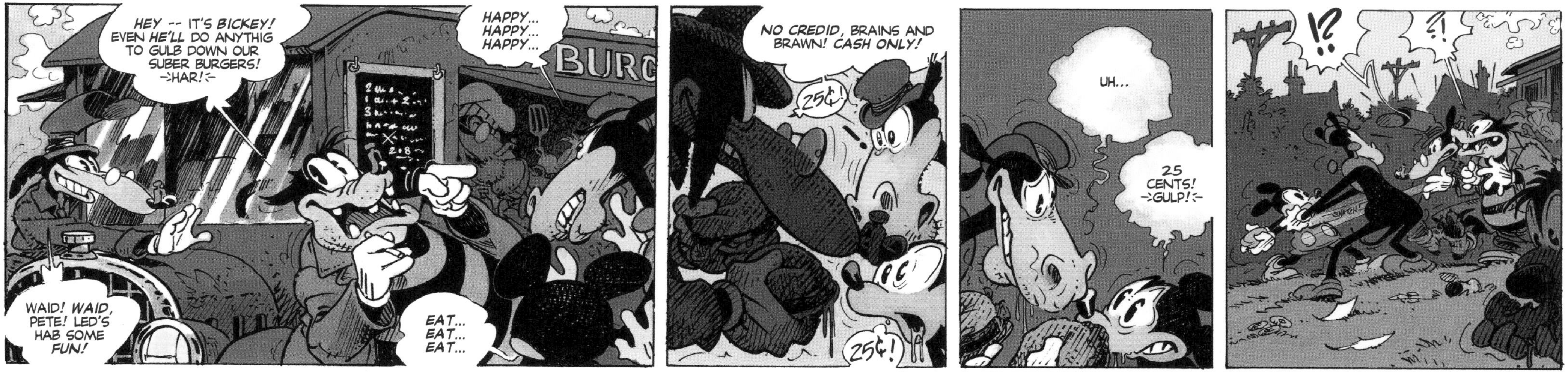
HEY -- IT'S BICKEY! EVEN HE'LL DO ANYTHIG TO GULB DOWN OUR SUBER BURGERS! -HAR!-
WAID! WAID, PETE! LED'S HAB SOME FUN!
HAPPY... HAPPY... HAPPY...
BURG
EAT... EAT... EAT...
NO CREDID, BRAINS AND BRAWN! CASH ONLY!
25¢!
25¢!
UH...
25 CENTS! -GULP!-
!?
?!

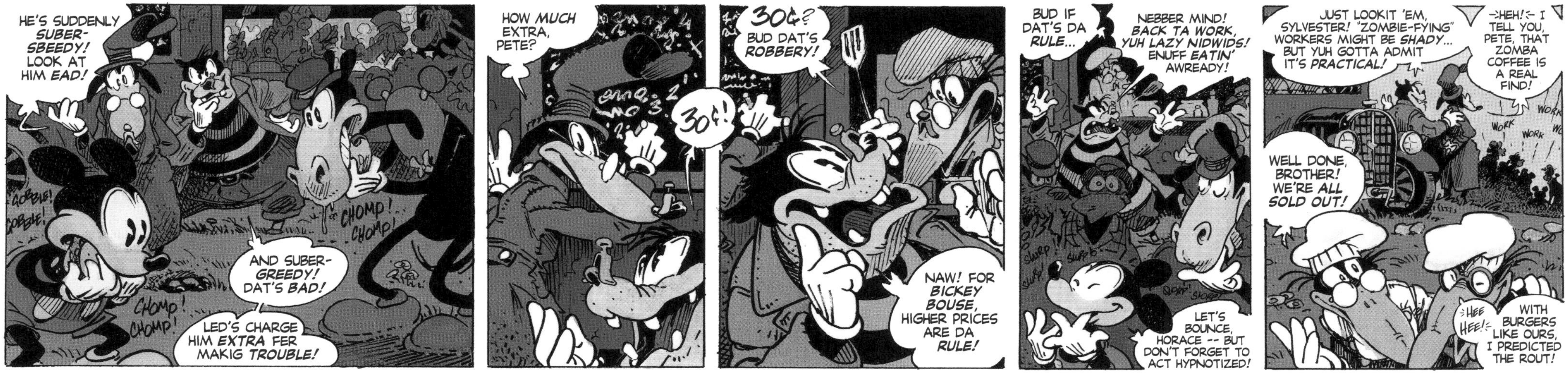
HE'S SUDDENLY SUBER-SBEEDY! LOOK AT HIM EAD!
GOBBLE! GOBBLE!
CHOMP! CHOMP!
CHOMP! CHOMP!
AND SUBER-GREEDY! DAT'S BAD!
LED'S CHARGE HIM EXTRA FER MAKIG TROUBLE!
HOW MUCH EXTRA, PETE?
30¢!
30¢? BUD DAT'S ROBBERY!
NAW! FOR BICKEY BOUSE, HIGHER PRICES ARE DA RULE!
BUD IF DAT'S DA RULE...
NEBBER MIND! BACK TA WORK, YUH LAZY NIDWIDS! ENUFF EATIN' AWREADY!
LET'S BOUNCE, HORACE -- BUT DON'T FORGET TO ACT HYPNOTIZED!
JUST LOOKIT 'EM, SYLVESTER! "ZOMBIE-FYING" WORKERS MIGHT BE SHADY... BUT YUH GOTTA ADMIT IT'S PRACTICAL!
-HEH!- I TELL YOU, PETE, THAT ZOMBA COFFEE IS A REAL FIND!
WORK WORK WORK WORK
WELL DONE, BROTHER! WE'RE ALL SOLD OUT!
HEE HEE!
WITH BURGERS LIKE OURS, I PREDICTED THE ROUT!

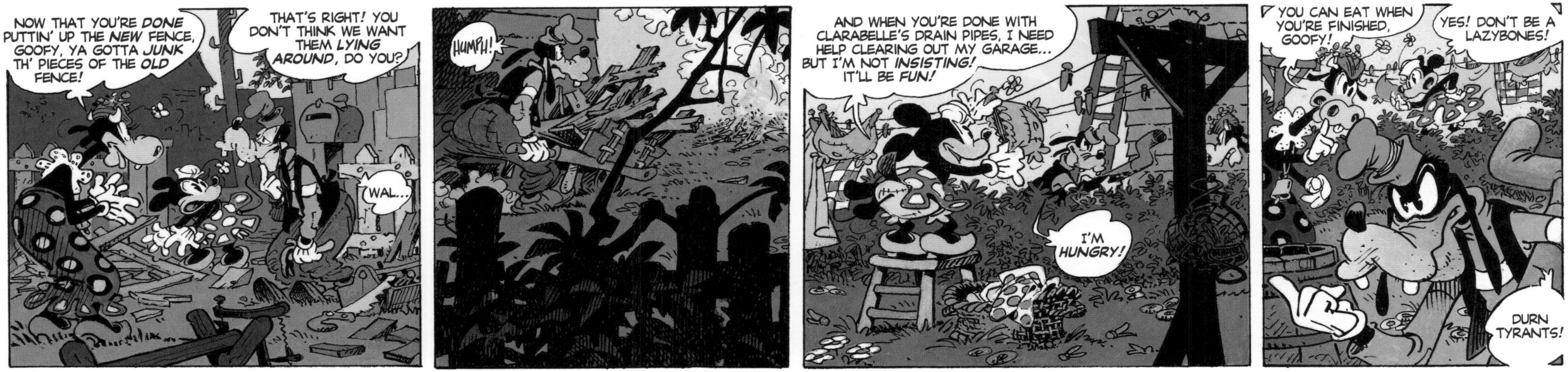
NOW THAT YOU'RE *DONE* PUTTIN' UP THE *NEW* FENCE, GOOFY, YA GOTTA *JUNK* TH' PIECES OF THE *OLD* FENCE!
THAT'S RIGHT! YOU DON'T THINK WE WANT THEM *LYING AROUND*, DO YOU?
WAL...
HUMPH!
AND WHEN YOU'RE DONE WITH CLARABELLE'S DRAIN PIPES, I NEED HELP CLEARING OUT MY GARAGE... BUT I'M NOT *INSISTING!* IT'LL BE *FUN!*
I'M *HUNGRY!*
YOU CAN EAT WHEN YOU'RE FINISHED, GOOFY!
YES! DON'T BE A LAZYBONES!
DURN TYRANTS!

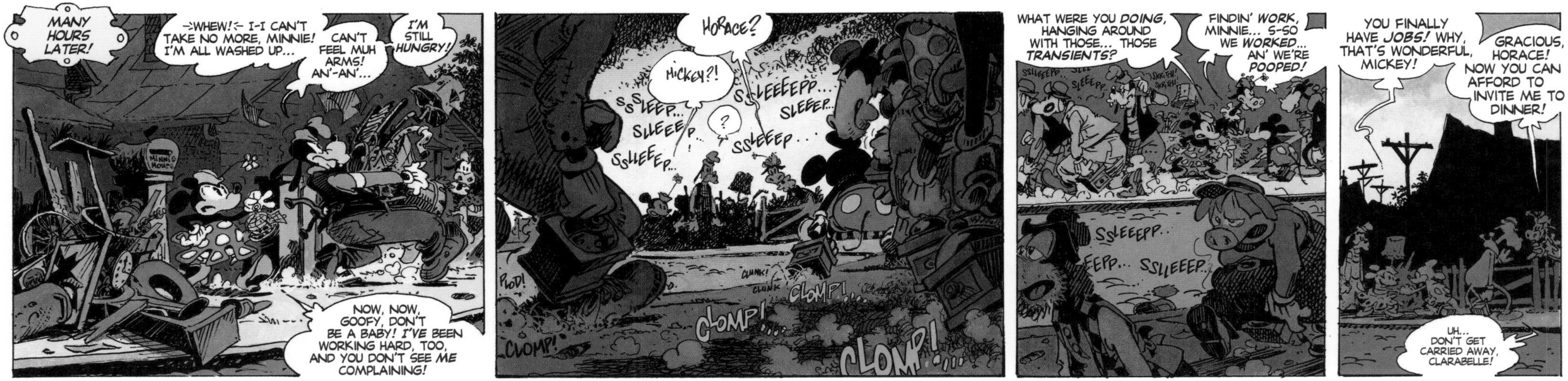
MANY HOURS LATER!
→WHEW!← I-I CAN'T TAKE NO MORE, MINNIE! I'M ALL WASHED UP...
CAN'T FEEL MUH ARMS! AN'-AN'...
I'M STILL *HUNGRY!*
NOW, NOW, GOOFY, DON'T BE A BABY! *I'VE* BEEN WORKING HARD, TOO, AND YOU DON'T SEE *ME* COMPLAINING!
HORACE?
MICKEY?!
SSSLEEP...
SLLEEEP...
SSLEEEP...
?
SSLEEEEPP...
SLEEEP...
SSLEEEP...
PLOD!
CLOMP!
CLUNK!
CLUNK
CLOMP!...
CLOMP!...
CLOMP!...
WHAT WERE YOU *DOING*, HANGING AROUND WITH THOSE... THOSE *TRANSIENTS?*
FINDIN' *WORK*, MINNIE... S-SO WE *WORKED*... AN' WE'RE *POOPED!*
SKRITCH! SKRITCH!
SSLEEEPP...
SLEEEPP...
SSLEEEPP...
EEPP...
SSLEEEP...
YOU FINALLY HAVE *JOBS!* WHY, THAT'S WONDERFUL, MICKEY!
GRACIOUS, HORACE! NOW YOU CAN AFFORD TO INVITE ME TO DINNER!
UH... DON'T GET CARRIED AWAY, CLARABELLE!

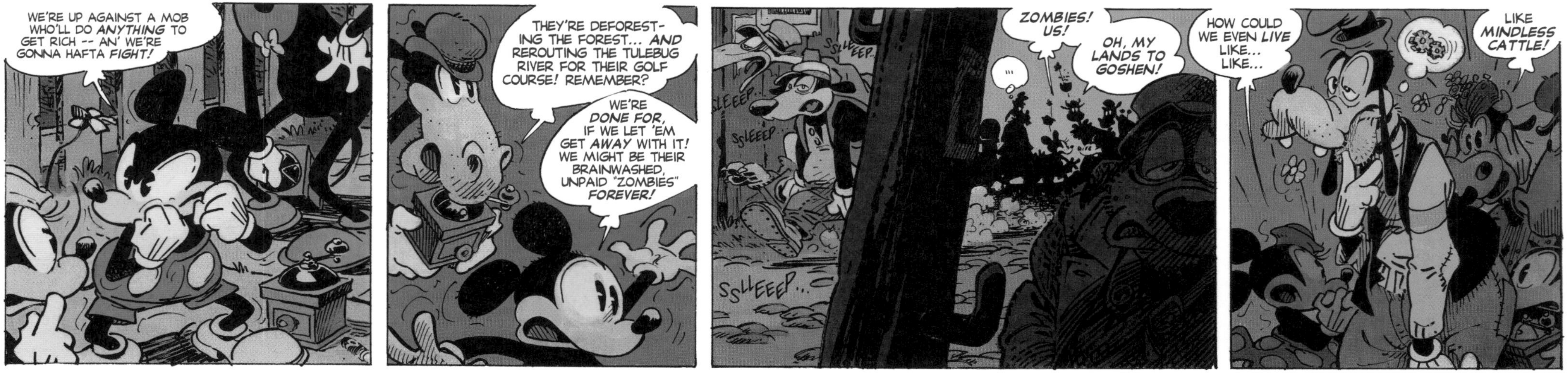
WE'RE UP AGAINST A MOB WHO'LL DO *ANYTHING* TO GET RICH -- AN' WE'RE GONNA HAFTA *FIGHT!*
THEY'RE DEFORESTING THE FOREST... *AND* REROUTING THE TULEBUG RIVER FOR THEIR GOLF COURSE! REMEMBER?
WE'RE *DONE FOR,* IF WE LET 'EM GET *AWAY* WITH IT! WE MIGHT BE THEIR BRAINWASHED, UNPAID "ZOMBIES" *FOREVER!*
SSLLEEEP..
SLEEEP...
SSLEEEP...
SSLLEEEP...
ZOMBIES! US!
OH, MY LANDS TO GOSHEN!
HOW COULD WE EVEN *LIVE* LIKE... LIKE...
LIKE *MINDLESS CATTLE!*

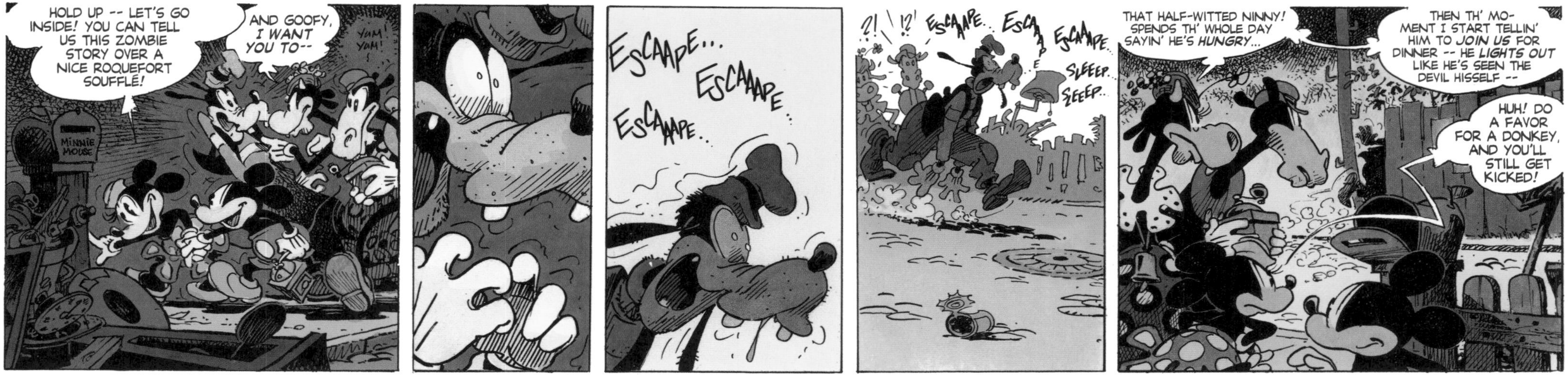
HOLD UP -- LET'S GO INSIDE! YOU CAN TELL US THIS ZOMBIE STORY OVER A NICE ROQUEFORT SOUFFLÉ!
AND GOOFY, *I WANT YOU TO--*
YUM YUM!
MINNIE MOUSE
ESCAAPE...
ESCAAAPE...
ESCAAAPE...
?!
!?
ESCAAAPE...
ESCAAAAPE
ESCAAAPE...
SLEEEP...
SLEEEP...
THAT HALF-WITTED NINNY! SPENDS TH' WHOLE DAY SAYIN' HE'S *HUNGRY*...
THEN TH' MOMENT I START TELLIN' HIM TO *JOIN US* FOR DINNER -- HE *LIGHTS OUT* LIKE HE'S SEEN THE DEVIL HISSELF --
HUH! DO A FAVOR FOR A DONKEY, AND YOU'LL STILL GET KICKED!

INSIDE! MICKEY AND HORACE TELL THE TALE FROM THE START! THINGS SOUND SILLY AT FIRST...

COFFEE?

WHAT? NOBODY THOUGHT OF MAKIN' TEA? ->TEE-HEE!<-

BUT MINNIE AND CLARABELLE ARE SOON SHOCKED BY WHAT THEY HEAR...

EEEEEK! MOO!

WHIPPING? LIKE MEDIEVAL PEASANTS?

->HMM!<- MAYBE THAT'D STRAIGHTEN GOOFY OUT!

...AND REPULSED BY THE VILLAINS' MACHIA-VELLIAN PLAN!

YAK! YAK!

THOSE POOR WORKERS, WITH NO BOX LUNCHES FROM HOME...

THEY'RE JUST LAZY, WITHOUT WIVES AN' KIDS TO COOK FOR 'EM! ->PFFT!<-

FINALLY: THE BURGERS! OUR BOYS DESCRIBE THEIR HYPNOTIC AROMA AND THEIR PAYCHECK-GOUGING PRICE! (BUT VERY LITTLE ABOUT THEIR TASTE!)

AN' THAT'S EVERYTHING, GIRLS!

GRACIOUS! SUCH A MESSY CRIMINAL PLOT -- WOULDN'T YOU SAY, CLARABELLE?

WHAT'CHA WANNA DO, MINNIE... TIDY IT UP?

OUR GANG HEADS HOME! NOT TIRED...

...BUT JUST GOOD OLD PHYSI-CALLY FA-TIGUED!

ZZZ

GAZAZZ... SNRF!

ZZZ ZAWP!

ZZZ

HELLO, CLARABELLE? IT'S ME! I'VE GOT IDEAS!

56

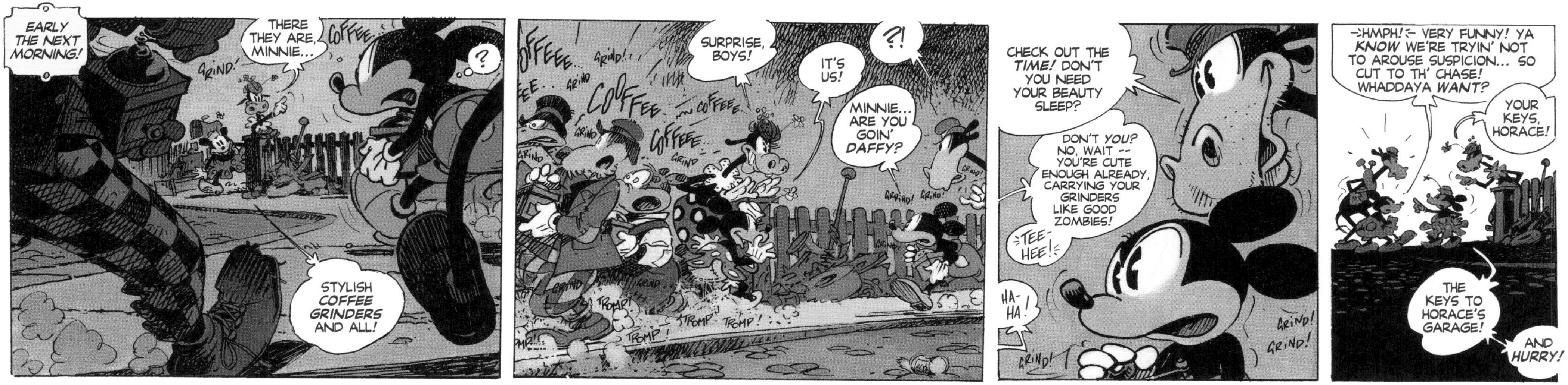
EARLY THE NEXT MORNING!
THERE THEY ARE, MINNIE...
COFFEE...
GRIND!
?
STYLISH COFFEE GRINDERS AND ALL!
COFFEEE... GRIND!
COFFEE... GRIND
SURPRISE, BOYS!
IT'S US!
?!
MINNIE... ARE YOU GOIN' DAFFY?
TROMP! TROMP! TROMP!
CHECK OUT THE TIME! DON'T YOU NEED YOUR BEAUTY SLEEP?
DON'T YOU? NO, WAIT -- YOU'RE CUTE ENOUGH ALREADY, CARRYING YOUR GRINDERS LIKE GOOD ZOMBIES!
TEE-HEE!
HA-HA!
GRIND!
GRIND! GRIND!
—HMPH!— VERY FUNNY! YA KNOW WE'RE TRYIN' NOT TO AROUSE SUSPICION... SO CUT TO TH' CHASE! WHADDAYA WANT?
YOUR KEYS, HORACE!
THE KEYS TO HORACE'S GARAGE!
AND HURRY!

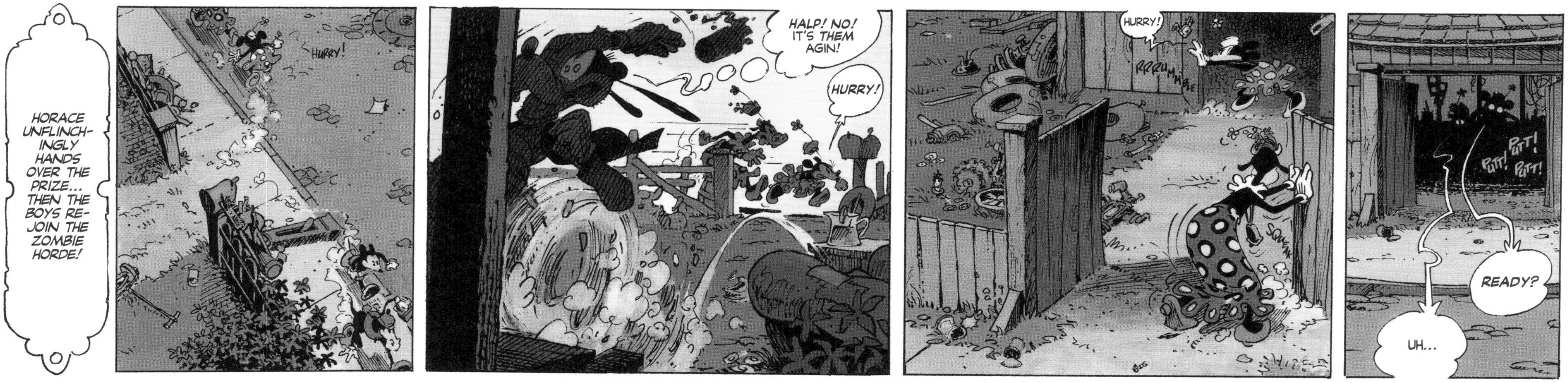
HORACE UNFLINCHINGLY HANDS OVER THE PRIZE... THEN THE BOYS REJOIN THE ZOMBIE HORDE!
HURRY!
HALP! NO! IT'S THEM AGIN!
HURRY!
HURRY!
RRRUMMBLE
SQUAWK
PUTT! PUTT! PUTT!
READY?
UH...

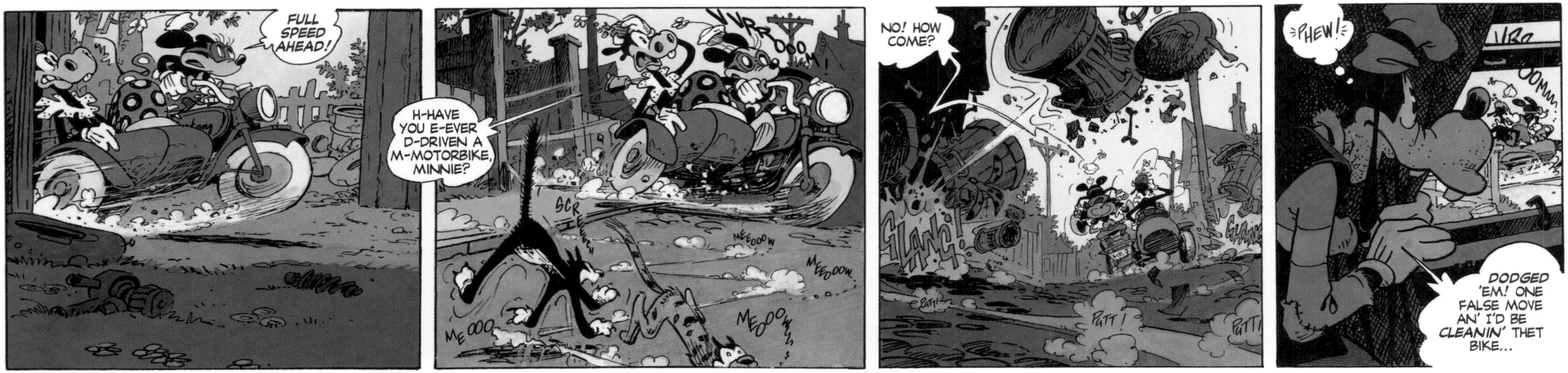
FULL SPEED AHEAD!
H-HAVE YOU E-EVER D-DRIVEN A M-MOTORBIKE, MINNIE?
MEOOO
MEOOOW
MEEOOOW
NO! HOW COME?
CLANG!
PUTT!
PHEW!
DODGED 'EM! ONE FALSE MOVE AN' I'D BE CLEANIN' THET BIKE...

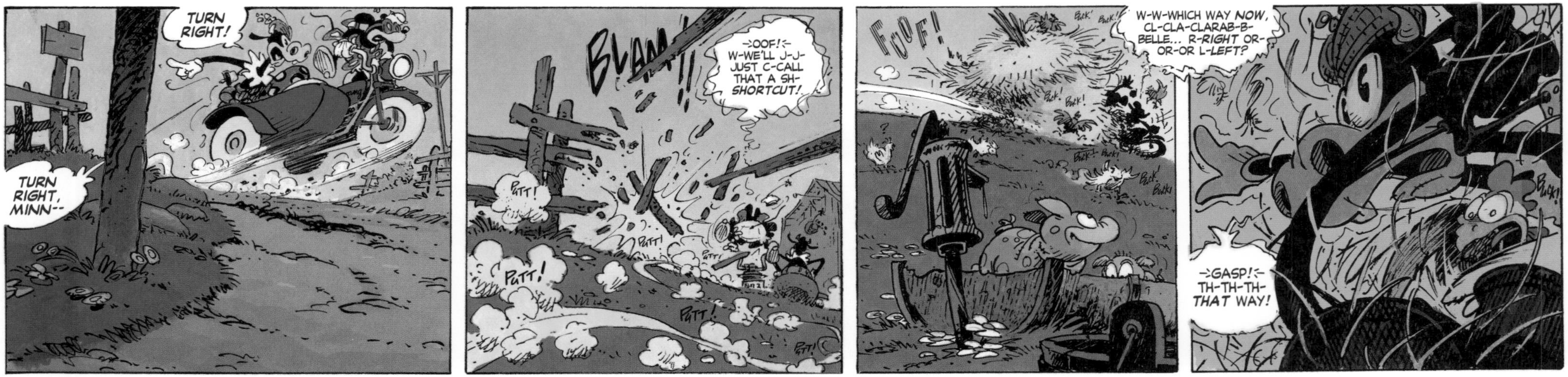
TURN RIGHT!
TURN RIGHT, MINN--
BLAM!!
-OOF!- W-WE'LL J-J-JUST C-CALL THAT A SH-SHORTCUT!
PUTT!
FOOF!
W-W-WHICH WAY NOW, CL-CLA-CLARAB-B-BELLE... R-RIGHT OR-OR-OR L-LEFT?
-GASP!- TH-TH-TH-THAT WAY!

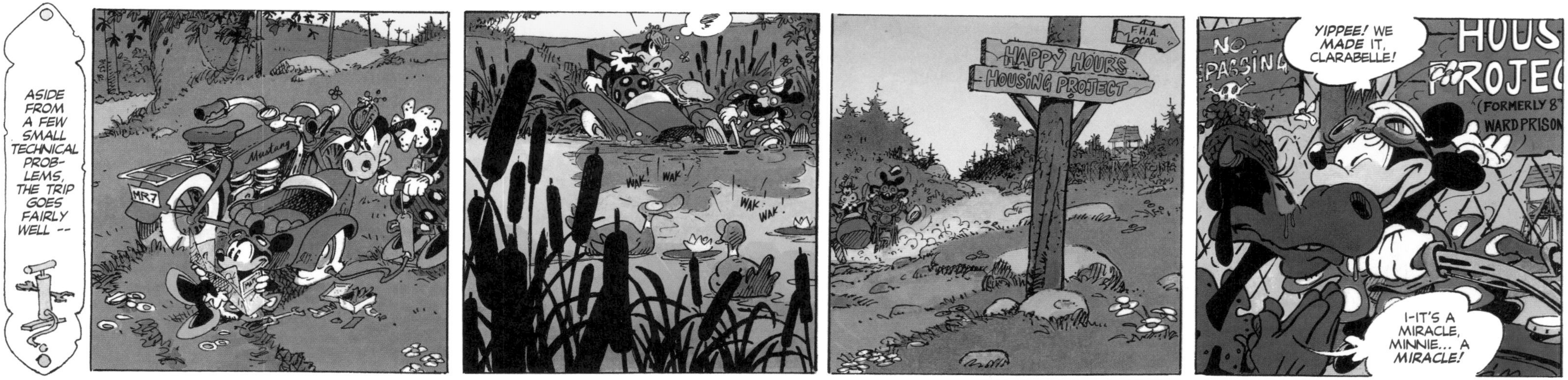

ASIDE FROM A FEW SMALL TECHNICAL PROBLEMS, THE TRIP GOES FAIRLY WELL --
Mustang
MR-7
WAK
WAK
WAK
WAK
HAPPY HOURS
HOUSING PROJECT
F.H.A. LOCAL
NO PASSING
YIPPEE! WE MADE IT, CLARABELLE!
HOUS
PROJEC
(FORMERLY 8TH
WARD PRISON
I-IT'S A MIRACLE, MINNIE... A MIRACLE!

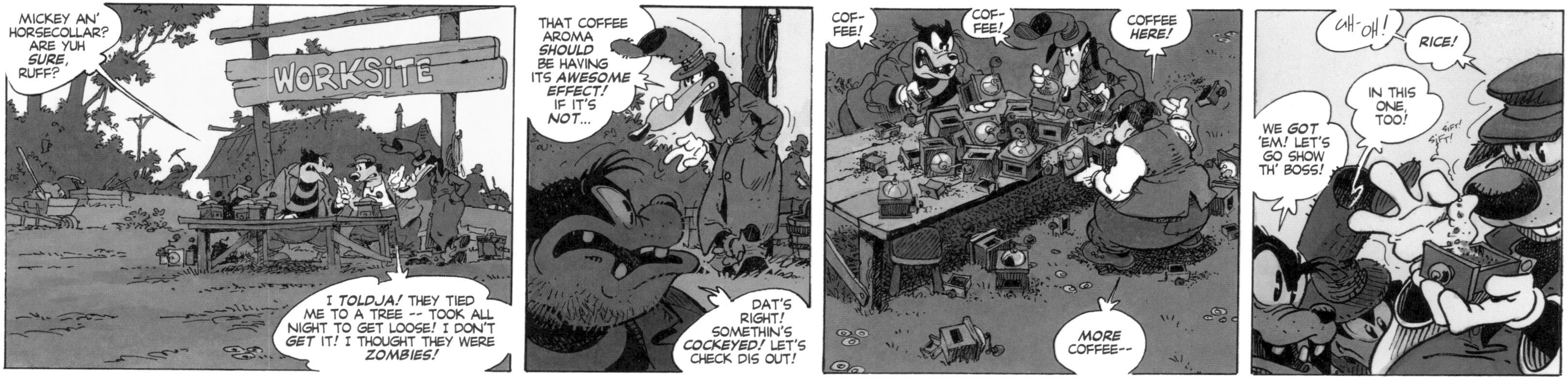

MICKEY AN' HORSECOLLAR? ARE YUH SURE, RUFF?
WORKSITE
I TOLDJA! THEY TIED ME TO A TREE -- TOOK ALL NIGHT TO GET LOOSE! I DON'T GET IT! I THOUGHT THEY WERE ZOMBIES!
THAT COFFEE AROMA SHOULD BE HAVING ITS AWESOME EFFECT! IF IT'S NOT...
DAT'S RIGHT! SOMETHIN'S COCKEYED! LET'S CHECK DIS OUT!
COF-FEE!
COF-FEE!
COFFEE HERE!
MORE COFFEE--
UH-OH!
RICE!
IN THIS ONE, TOO!
WE GOT 'EM! LET'S GO SHOW TH' BOSS!
SIFT! SIFT!

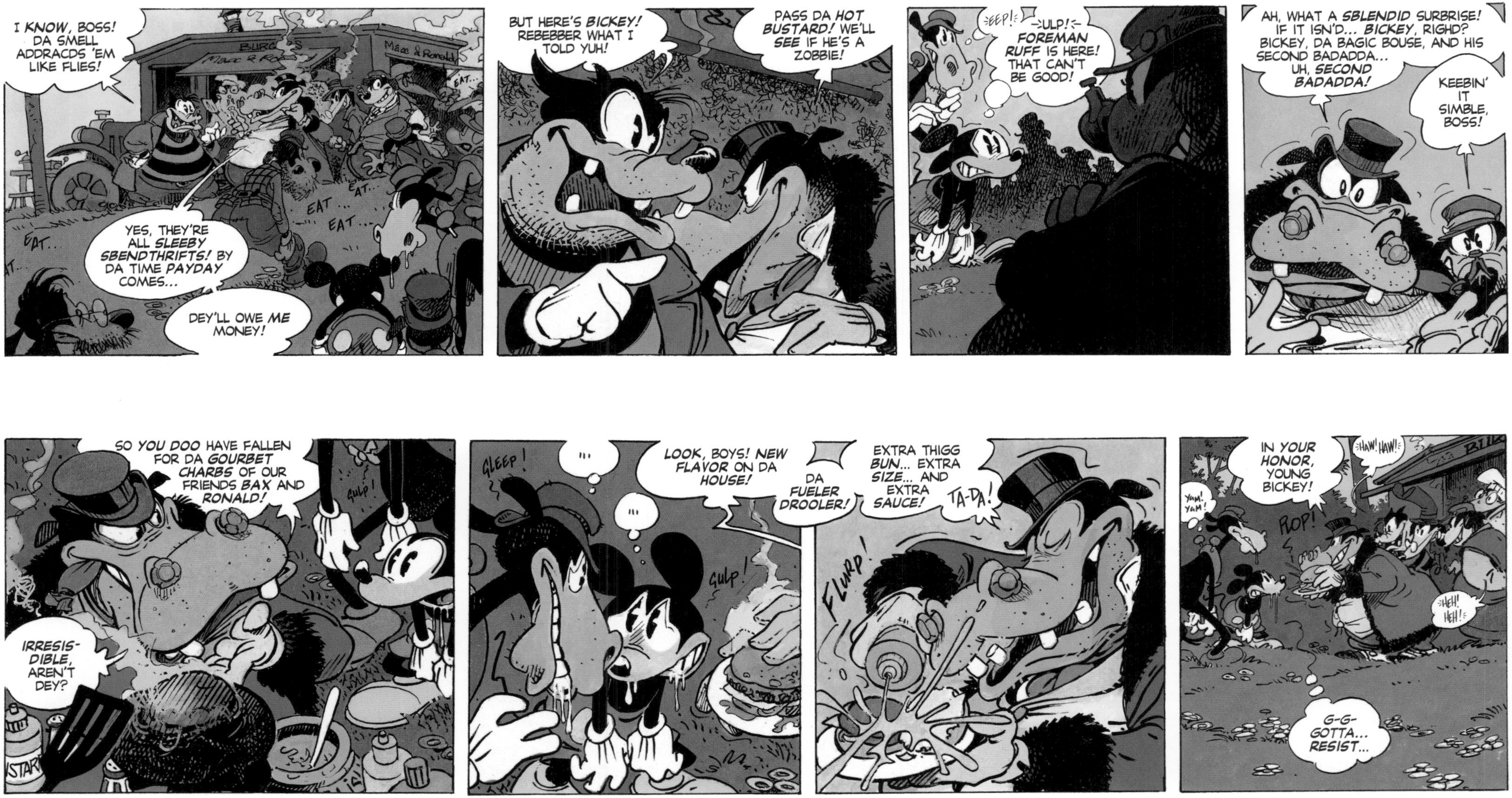

I KNOW, BOSS! DA SMELL ADDRACDS 'EM LIKE FLIES!
EAT...
EAT...
EAT...
EAT...
YES, THEY'RE ALL SLEEBY SBENDTHRIFTS! BY DA TIME PAYDAY COMES...
DEY'LL OWE ME MONEY!
BUT HERE'S BICKEY! REBEBBER WHAT I TOLD YUH!
PASS DA HOT BUSTARD! WE'LL SEE IF HE'S A ZOBBIE!
EEP!
ULP! FOREMAN RUFF IS HERE! THAT CAN'T BE GOOD!
AH, WHAT A SBLENDID SURBRISE! IF IT ISN'D... BICKEY, RIGHD? BICKEY, DA BAGIC BOUSE, AND HIS SECOND BADADDA... UH, SECOND BADADDA!
KEEBIN' IT SIMBLE, BOSS!
SO YOU DOO HAVE FALLEN FOR DA GOURBET CHARBS OF OUR FRIENDS BAX AND RONALD!
GULP
IRRESIS-DIBLE, AREN'T DEY?
GLEEP!
...
...
GULP!
LOOK, BOYS! NEW FLAVOR ON DA HOUSE!
DA FUELER DROOLER!
EXTRA THIGG BUN... EXTRA SIZE... AND EXTRA SAUCE!
TA-DA!
FLURP
IN YOUR HONOR, YOUNG BICKEY!
HAW! HAW!
YAM! YAM!
PLOP!
HEH! HEH!
G-G-GOTTA... RESIST...

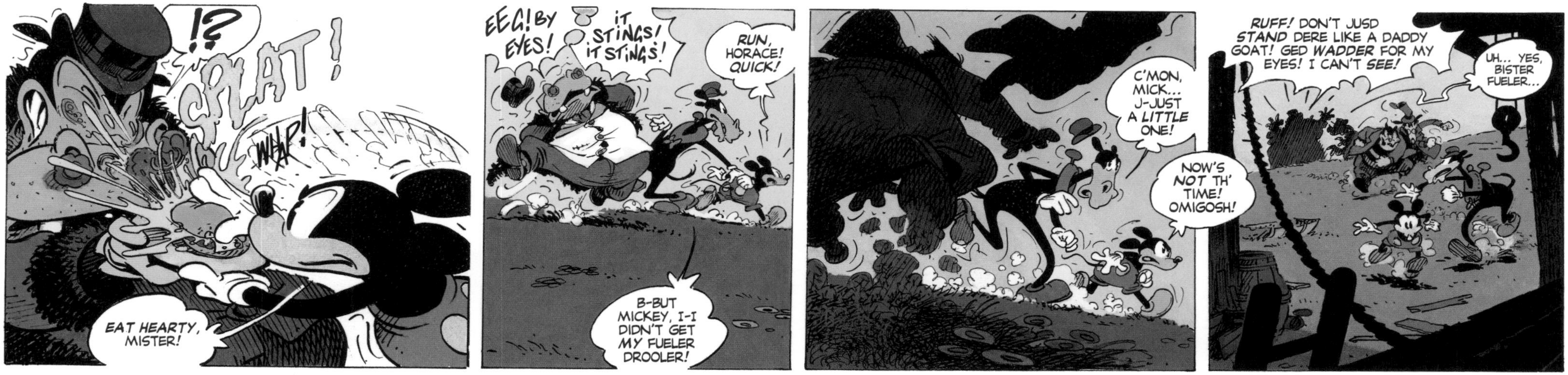
!?
SPLAT!
WHAP!
EAT HEARTY, MISTER!
EEG! BY EYES!
IT STINGS! IT STINGS!
RUN, HORACE! QUICK!
B-BUT MICKEY, I-I DIDN'T GET MY FUELER DROOLER!
C'MON, MICK... J-JUST A LITTLE ONE!
NOW'S NOT TH' TIME! OMIGOSH!
RUFF! DON'T JUSD STAND DERE LIKE A DADDY GOAT! GED WADDER FOR MY EYES! I CAN'T SEE!
UH... YES, BISTER FUELER...

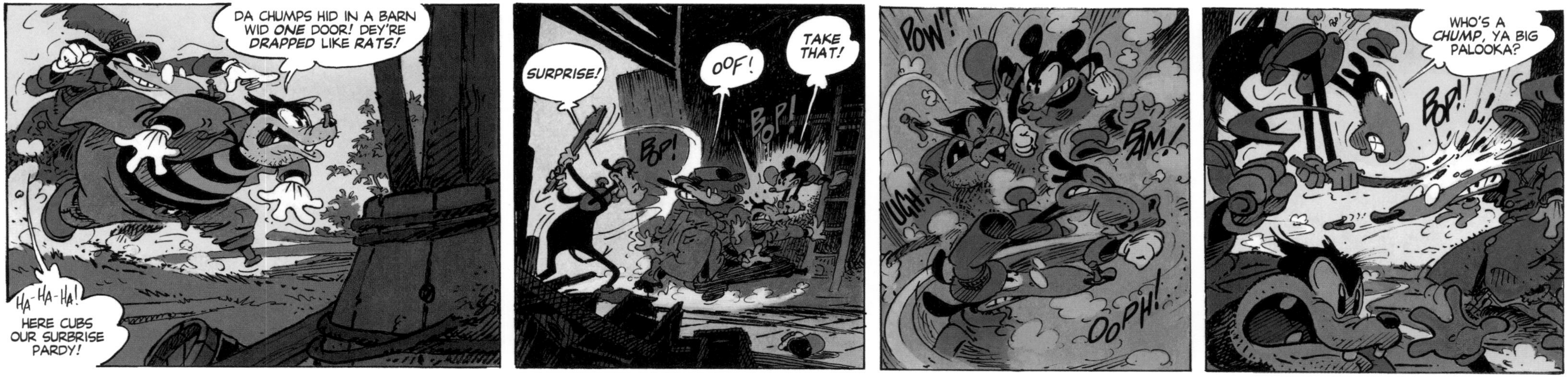
DA CHUMPS HID IN A BARN WID ONE DOOR! DEY'RE DRAPPED LIKE RATS!
HA-HA-HA! HERE CUBS OUR SURBRISE PARDY!
SURPRISE!
BOP!
OOF!
BOP!
TAKE THAT!
POW!
UGH!
BAM!
OOPH!
BOP!
WHO'S A CHUMP, YA BIG PALOOKA?

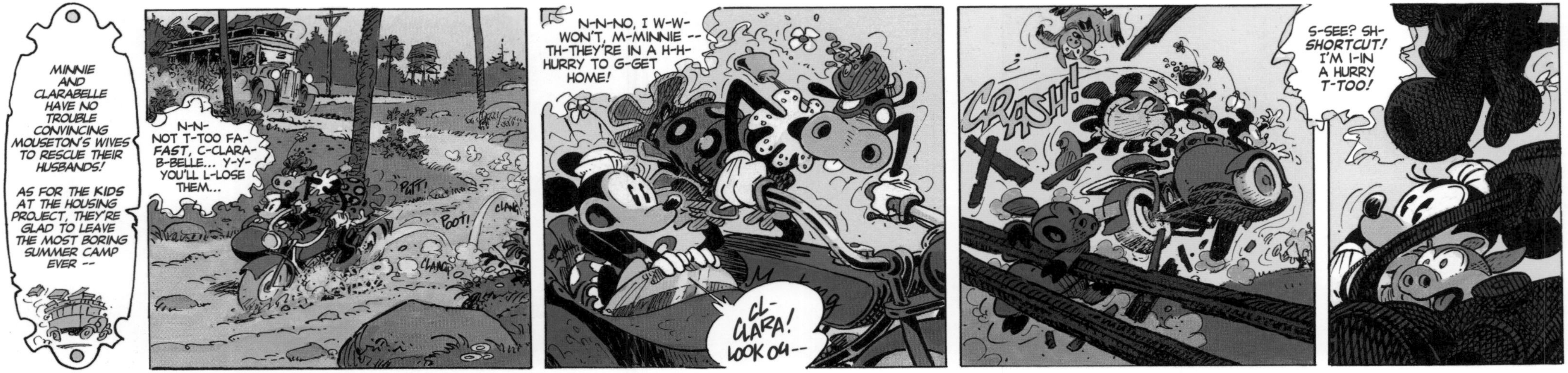
MINNIE AND CLARABELLE HAVE NO TROUBLE CONVINCING MOUSETON'S WIVES TO RESCUE THEIR HUSBANDS!
AS FOR THE KIDS AT THE HOUSING PROJECT, THEY'RE GLAD TO LEAVE THE MOST BORING SUMMER CAMP EVER --
N-N-NOT T-TOO FA-FAST, C-CLARA-B-BELLE... Y-Y-YOU'LL L-LOSE THEM...
PUTT!
POOT!
CLANG!
CLANG!
N-N-NO, I W-W-WON'T, M-MINNIE -- TH-THEY'RE IN A H-H-HURRY TO G-GET HOME!
CL-CLARA! LOOK OU--
CRASH!
S-SEE? SH-SHORTCUT! I'M I-IN A HURRY T-TOO!

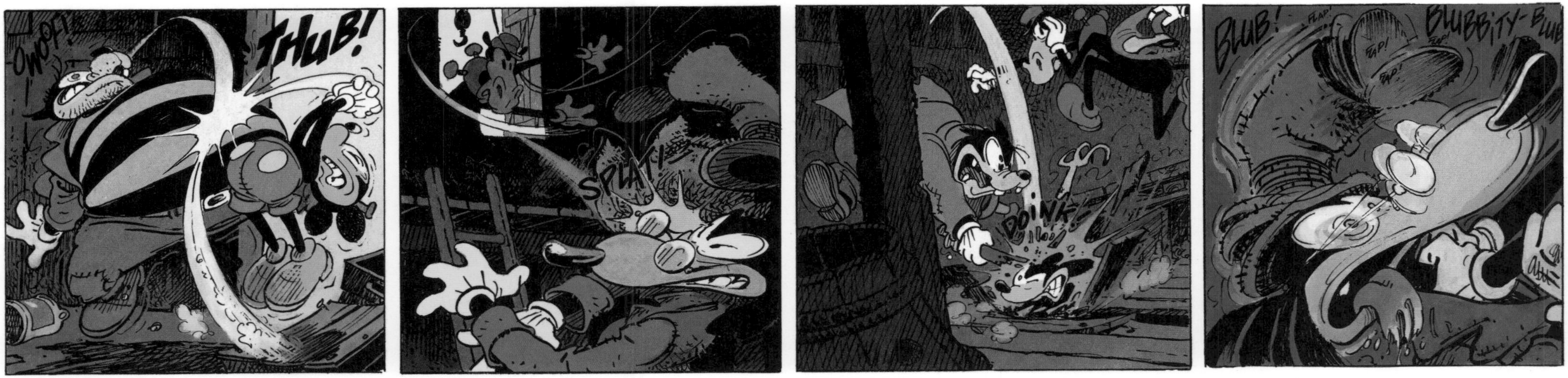
OWOOF!
THUB!
SPLAT!
DOINK!
BLUB!
FLAP!
FLAP!
FLAP!
BLUBBITY-BLUB

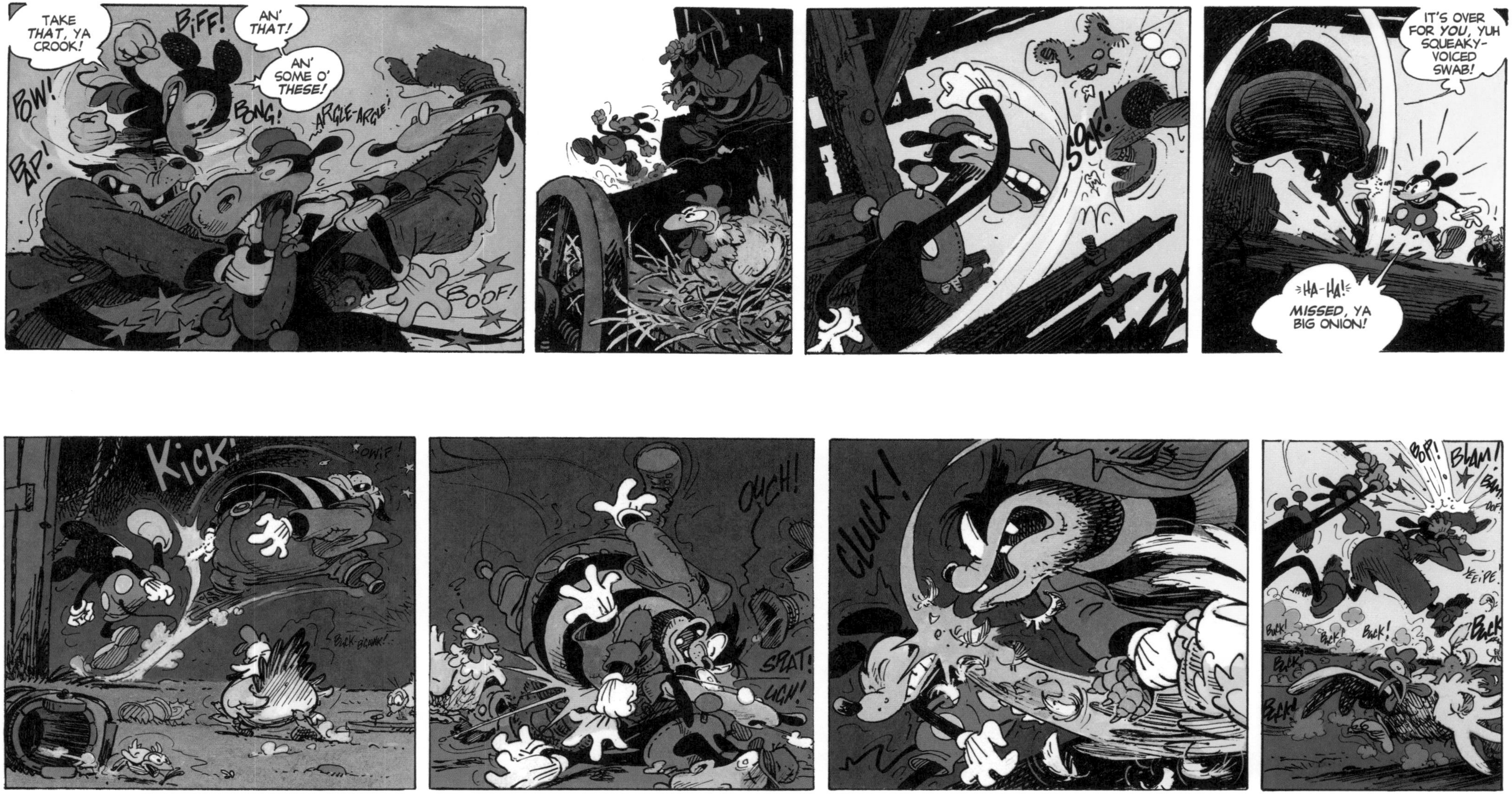
TAKE THAT, YA CROOK!
BIFF!
AN' THAT!
AN' SOME O' THESE!
POW!
BAP!
BONG!
ARGLE-ARGLE!
BOOF!
SOCK!
IT'S OVER FOR YOU, YUH SQUEAKY-VOICED SWAB!
HA-HA! MISSED, YA BIG ONION!
KICK!
OUCH!
SPLAT!
UGH!
CLUCK!
BOP!
BLAM!
BUCK!

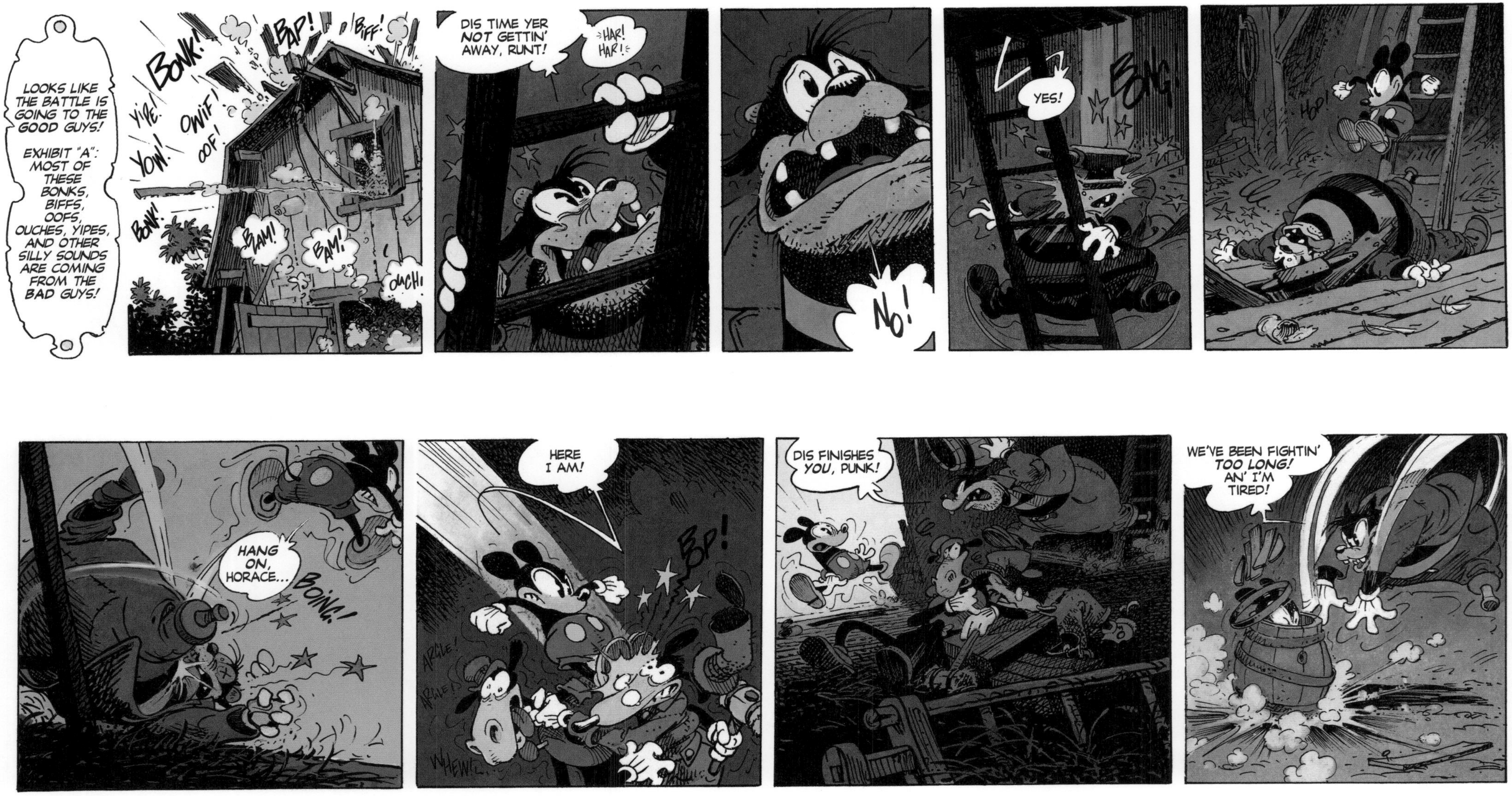
LOOKS LIKE THE BATTLE IS GOING TO THE GOOD GUYS!
EXHIBIT "A": MOST OF THESE BONKS, BIFFS, OOFS, OUCHES, YIPES, AND OTHER SILLY SOUNDS ARE COMING FROM THE BAD GUYS!
BONK!
BAP!
BIFF!
YIPE!
OWIF!
YOW!
OOF!
BONK!
BAM!
BAM!
OUCH!
DIS TIME YER NOT GETTIN' AWAY, RUNT!
HAR! HAR!
NO!
YES!
BONG!
HOP!
HANG ON, HORACE...
BOING!
HERE I AM!
BOP!
ARGLE!
ARGLE!
WHEW!
DIS FINISHES YOU, PUNK!
WE'VE BEEN FIGHTIN' TOO LONG! AN' I'M TIRED!

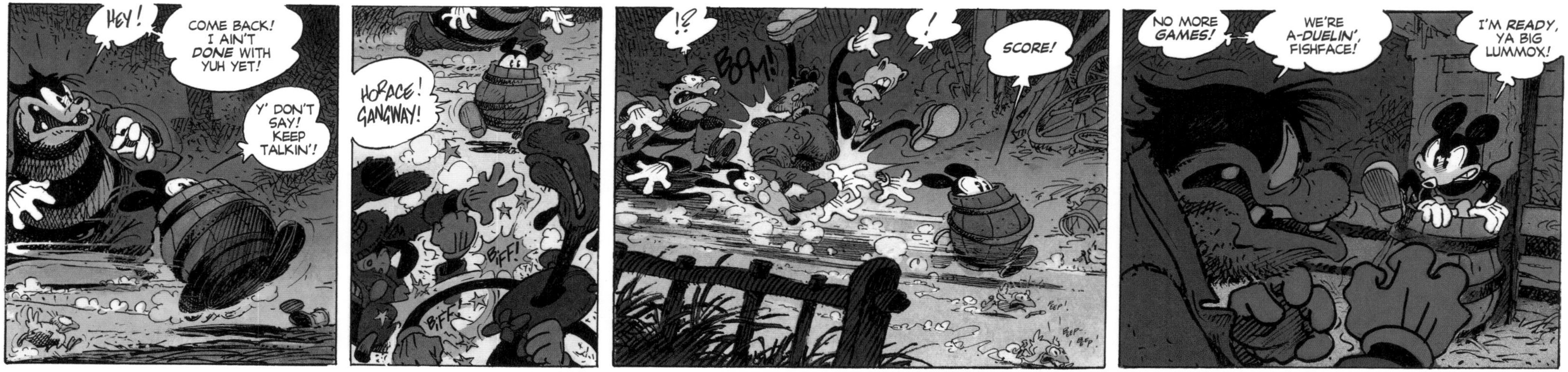
HEY!
COME BACK! I AIN'T DONE WITH YUH YET!
Y' DON'T SAY! KEEP TALKIN'!
HORACE! GANGWAY!
BIFF!
BIFF!
!?
BOOM!
!
SCORE!
NO MORE GAMES!
WE'RE A-DUELIN', FISHFACE!
I'M READY, YA BIG LUMMOX!

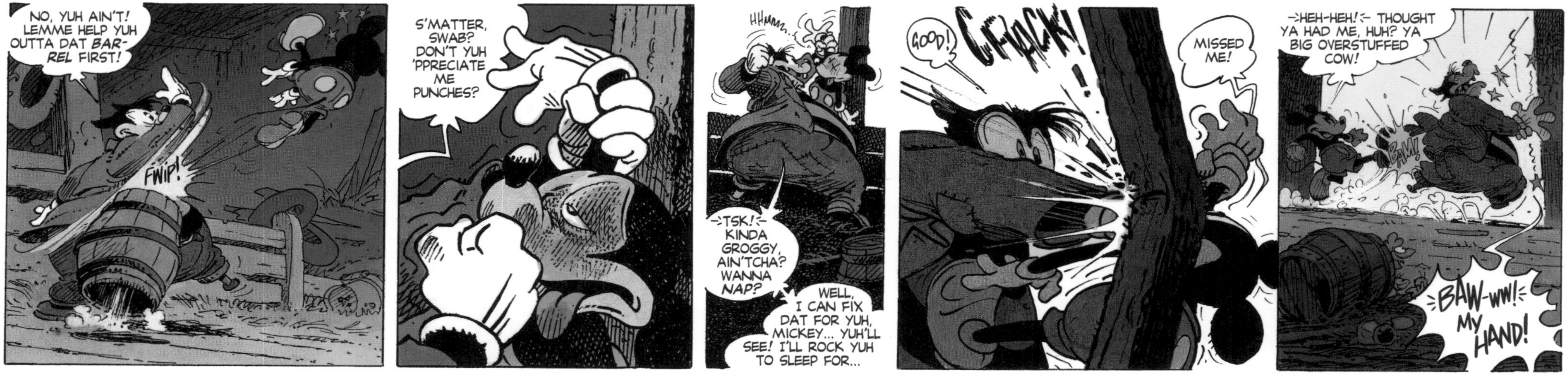
NO, YUH AIN'T! LEMME HELP YUH OUTTA DAT BAR-REL FIRST!
FWIP!
S'MATTER, SWAB? DON'T YUH 'PPRECIATE ME PUNCHES?
-TSK!- KINDA GROGGY, AIN'TCHA? WANNA NAP?
WELL, I CAN FIX DAT FOR YUH, MICKEY... YUH'LL SEE! I'LL ROCK YUH TO SLEEP FOR...
GOOD!
CRACK!
MISSED ME!
-HEH-HEH!- THOUGHT YA HAD ME, HUH? YA BIG OVERSTUFFED COW!
BAM!
BAW-WW! MY HAND!

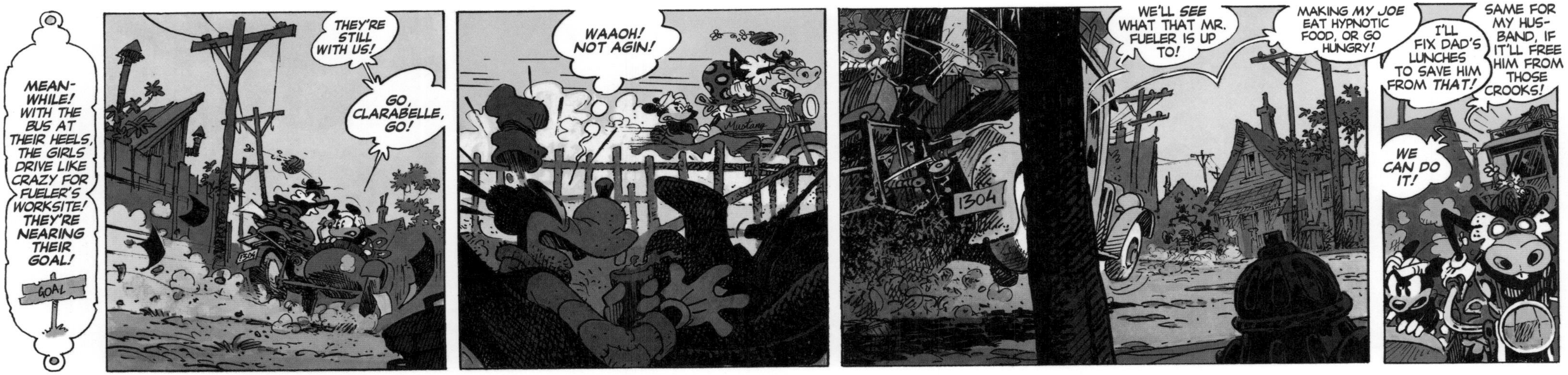
MEAN-WHILE! WITH THE BUS AT THEIR HEELS, THE GIRLS DRIVE LIKE CRAZY FOR FUELER'S WORKSITE! THEY'RE NEARING THEIR GOAL!
GOAL
THEY'RE STILL WITH US!
GO, CLARABELLE, GO!
WAAOH! NOT AGIN!
Mustang
1304
WE'LL SEE WHAT THAT MR. FUELER IS UP TO!
MAKING MY JOE EAT HYPNOTIC FOOD, OR GO HUNGRY!
I'LL FIX DAD'S LUNCHES TO SAVE HIM FROM THAT!
SAME FOR MY HUS-BAND, IF IT'LL FREE HIM FROM THOSE CROOKS!
WE CAN DO IT!

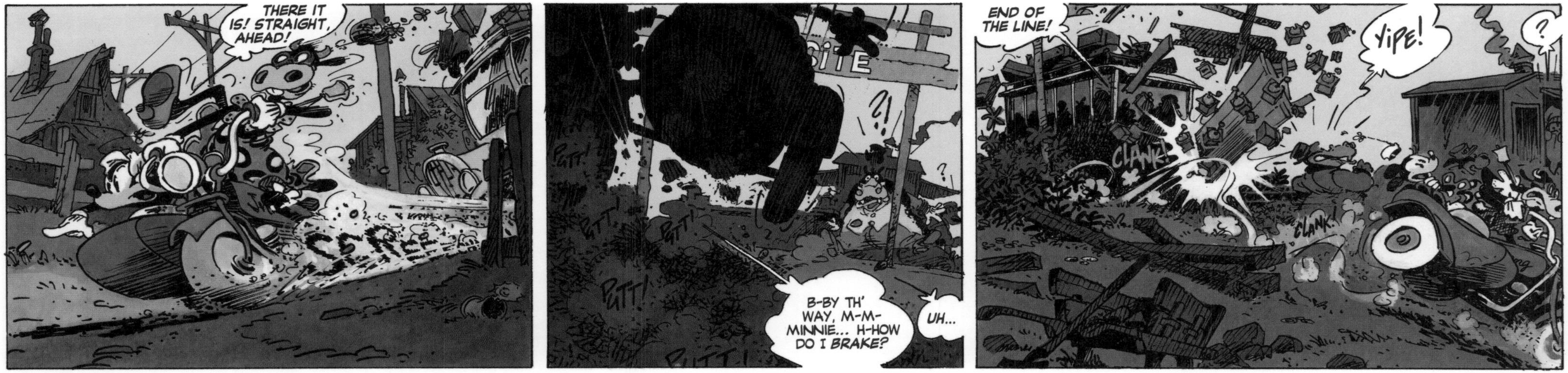
THERE IT IS! STRAIGHT AHEAD!
SITE
?!
PUTT!
PUTT!
PUTT!
B-BY TH' WAY, M-M-MINNIE... H-HOW DO I BRAKE?
UH...
END OF THE LINE!
YIPE!
?
CLANK!
CLANK.

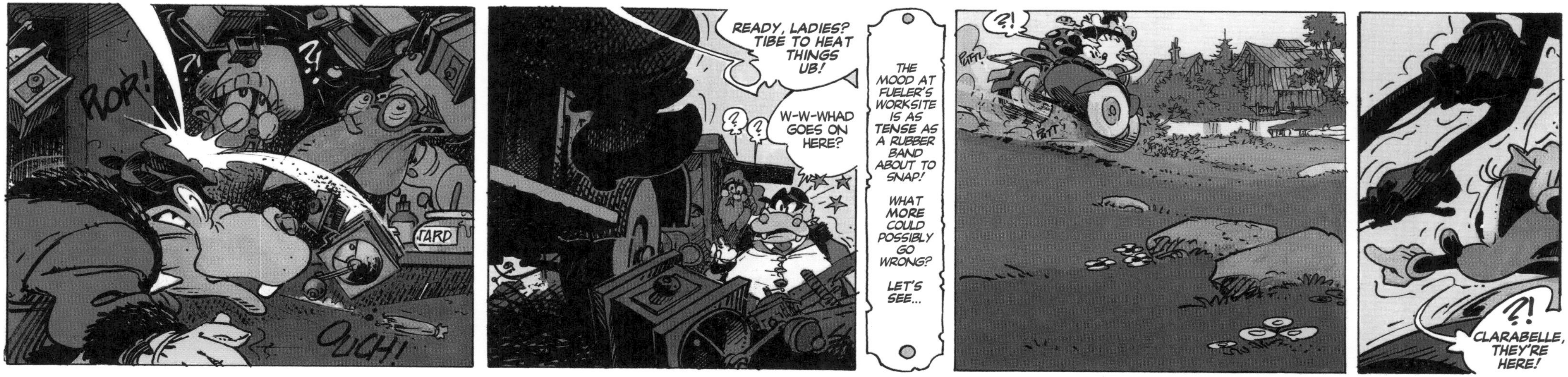
?!
?!
ROR!
OUCH!
READY, LADIES? TIBE TO HEAT THINGS UB!
?
?
W-W-WHAD GOES ON HERE?
THE MOOD AT FUELER'S WORKSITE IS AS TENSE AS A RUBBER BAND ABOUT TO SNAP!
WHAT MORE COULD POSSIBLY GO WRONG?
LET'S SEE...
?!
?!
CLARABELLE, THEY'RE HERE!

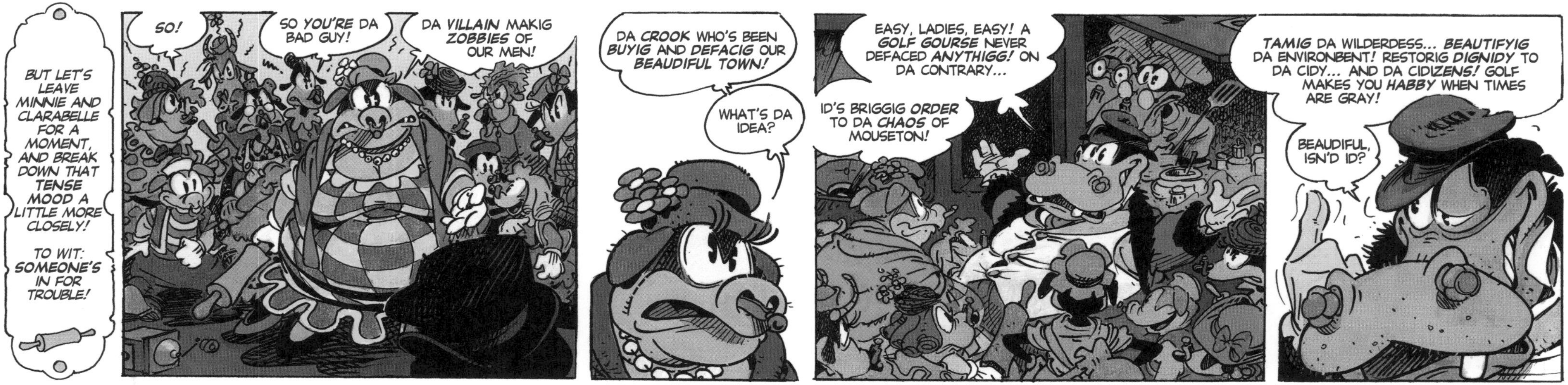
BUT LET'S LEAVE MINNIE AND CLARABELLE FOR A MOMENT, AND BREAK DOWN THAT TENSE MOOD A LITTLE MORE CLOSELY!
TO WIT: SOMEONE'S IN FOR TROUBLE!
SO!
SO YOU'RE DA BAD GUY!
DA VILLAIN MAKIG ZOBBIES OF OUR MEN!
DA CROOK WHO'S BEEN BUYIG AND DEFACIG OUR BEAUDIFUL TOWN!
WHAT'S DA IDEA?
EASY, LADIES, EASY! A GOLF GOURSE NEVER DEFACED ANYTHIGG! ON DA CONTRARY...
ID'S BRIGGIG ORDER TO DA CHAOS OF MOUSETON!
TAMIG DA WILDERDESS... BEAUTIFYIG DA ENVIRONBENT! RESTORIG DIGNIDY TO DA CIDY... AND DA CIDIZENS! GOLF MAKES YOU HABBY WHEN TIMES ARE GRAY!
BEAUDIFUL, ISN'D ID?

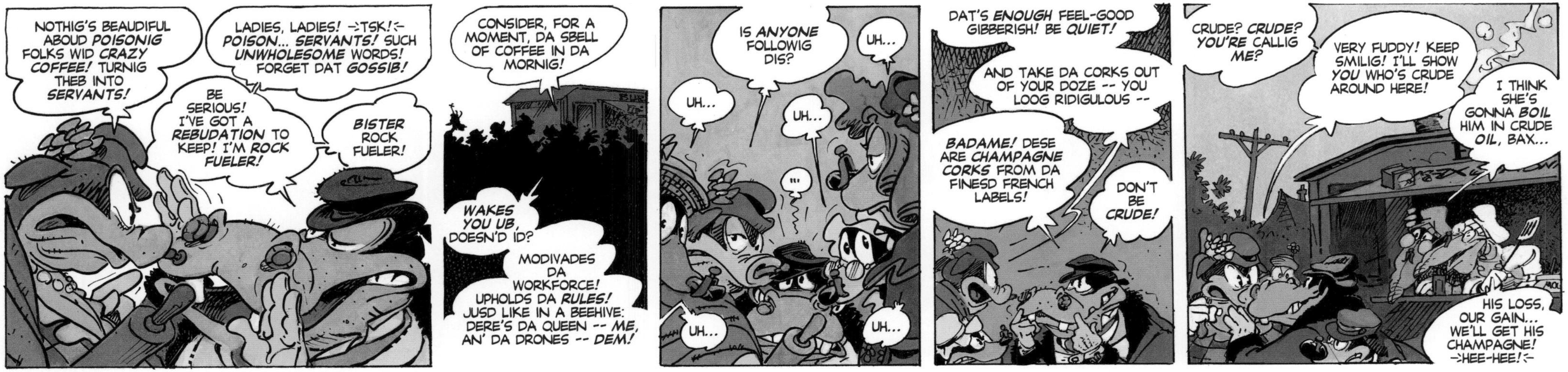
NOTHIG'S BEAUDIFUL ABOUD POISONIG FOLKS WID CRAZY COFFEE! TURNIG THEB INTO SERVANTS!
LADIES, LADIES! -TSK!- POISON... SERVANTS! SUCH UNWHOLESOME WORDS! FORGET DAT GOSSIB!
BE SERIOUS! I'VE GOT A REBUDATION TO KEEP! I'M ROCK FUELER!
BISTER ROCK FUELER!
CONSIDER, FOR A MOMENT, DA SBELL OF COFFEE IN DA MORNIG!
WAKES YOU UB, DOESN'D ID?
MODIVADES DA WORKFORCE!
UPHOLDS DA RULES! JUSD LIKE IN A BEEHIVE: DERE'S DA QUEEN -- ME, AN' DA DRONES -- DEM!
IS ANYONE FOLLOWIG DIS?
UH...
UH...
UH...
...
UH...
UH...
DAT'S ENOUGH FEEL-GOOD GIBBERISH! BE QUIET!
AND TAKE DA CORKS OUT OF YOUR DOZE -- YOU LOOG RIDIGULOUS --
BADAME! DESE ARE CHAMPAGNE CORKS FROM DA FINESD FRENCH LABELS!
DON'T BE CRUDE!
CRUDE? CRUDE? YOU'RE CALLIG ME?
VERY FUDDY! KEEP SMILIG! I'LL SHOW YOU WHO'S CRUDE AROUND HERE!
I THINK SHE'S GONNA BOIL HIM IN CRUDE OIL, BAX...
HIS LOSS, OUR GAIN... WE'LL GET HIS CHAMPAGNE! -HEE-HEE!-

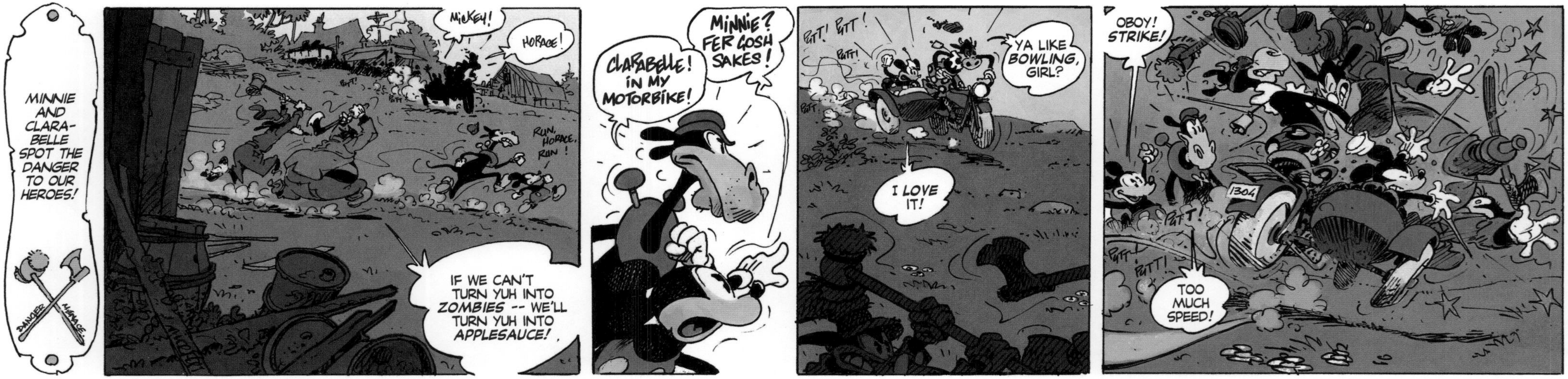
MINNIE AND CLARA-BELLE SPOT THE DANGER TO OUR HEROES!
DANGER
MENACE
MICKEY!
HORACE!
RUN, HORACE, RUN!
IF WE CAN'T TURN YUH INTO ZOMBIES -- WE'LL TURN YUH INTO APPLESAUCE!
CLARABELLE! IN MY MOTORBIKE!
MINNIE? FER GOSH SAKES!
PUTT! PUTT!
PUTT!
YA LIKE BOWLING, GIRL?
I LOVE IT!
OBOY! STRIKE!
1304
PUTT!
TOO MUCH SPEED!

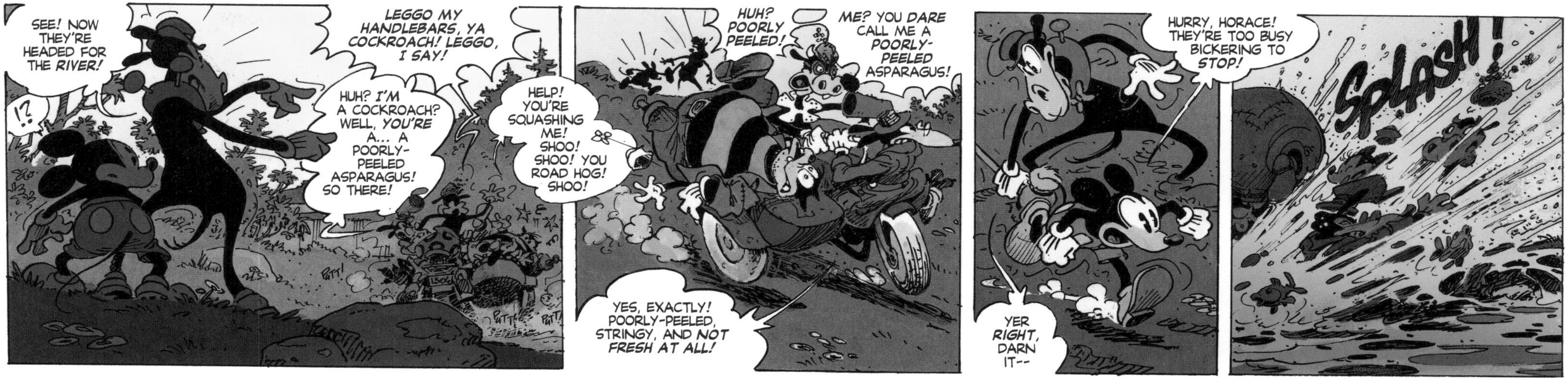

SEE! NOW THEY'RE HEADED FOR THE RIVER!
!?
LEGGO MY HANDLEBARS, YA COCKROACH! LEGGO, I SAY!
HUH? I'M A COCKROACH? WELL, YOU'RE A... A POORLY-PEELED ASPARAGUS! SO THERE!
HELP! YOU'RE SQUASHING ME! SHOO! SHOO! YOU ROAD HOG! SHOO!
PUTT!
PUTT!
PUTT!
HUH? POORLY PEELED!
ME? YOU DARE CALL ME A POORLY-PEELED ASPARAGUS!
YES, EXACTLY! POORLY-PEELED, STRINGY, AND NOT FRESH AT ALL!
HURRY, HORACE! THEY'RE TOO BUSY BICKERING TO STOP!
YER RIGHT, DARN IT--
SPLASH!

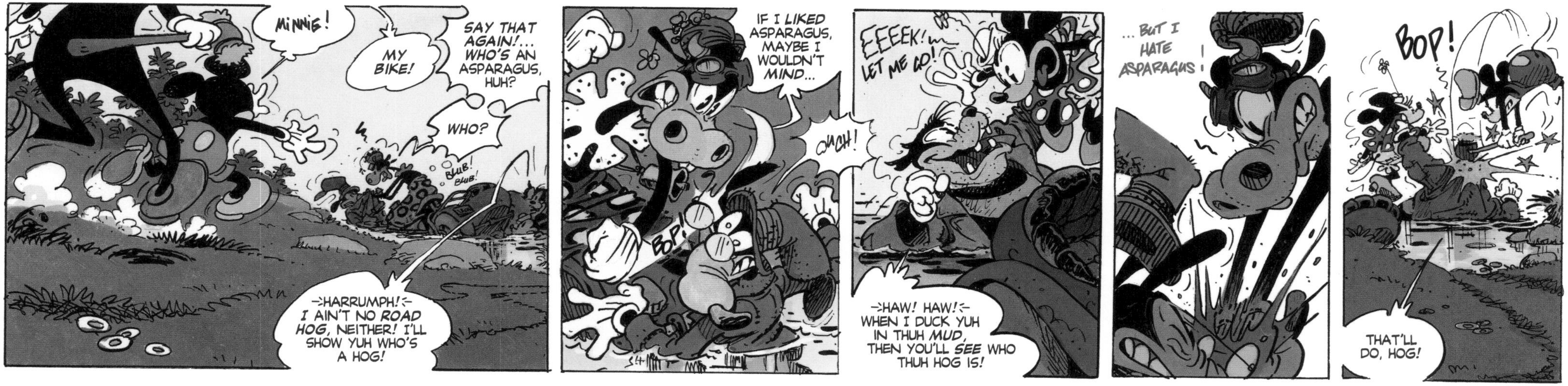

MINNIE!
MY BIKE!
SAY THAT AGAIN!... WHO'S AN ASPARAGUS, HUH?
WHO?
BLUB! BLUB!
—HARRUMPH!— I AIN'T NO ROAD HOG, NEITHER! I'LL SHOW YUH WHO'S A HOG!
IF I LIKED ASPARAGUS, MAYBE I WOULDN'T MIND...
OUCH!
BOP!
EEEEK! LET ME GO!
—HAW! HAW!— WHEN I DUCK YUH IN THUH MUD, THEN YOU'LL SEE WHO THUH HOG IS!
... BUT I HATE ASPARAGUS!
BOP!
THAT'LL DO, HOG!

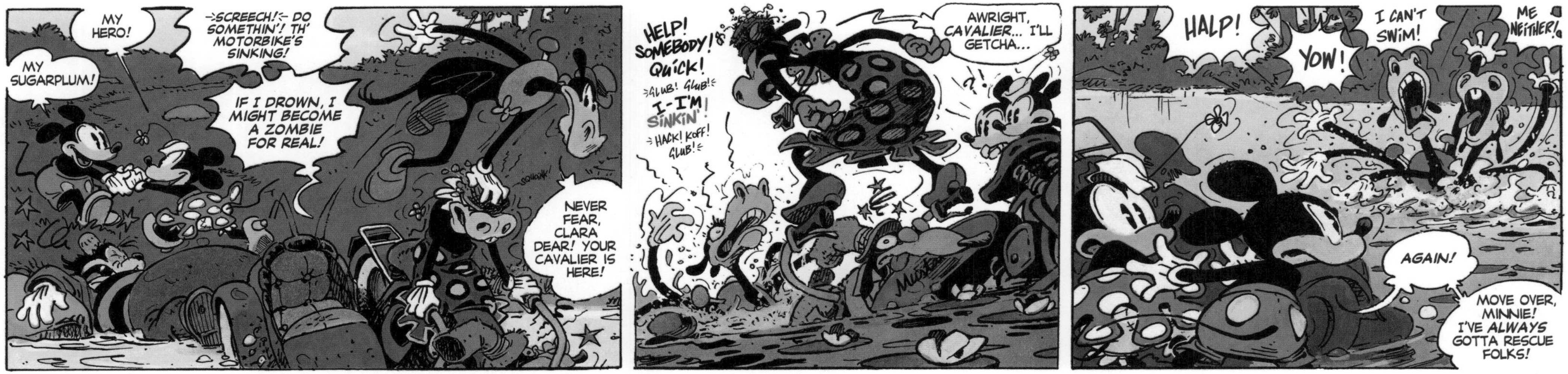
MY HERO!
MY SUGARPLUM!
SCREECH! DO SOMETHIN'! TH' MOTORBIKE'S SINKING!
IF I DROWN, I MIGHT BECOME A ZOMBIE FOR REAL!
NEVER FEAR, CLARA DEAR! YOUR CAVALIER IS HERE!
HELP! SOMEBODY! QUICK!
GLUB! GLUB!
I-I'M SINKIN'!
HACK! KOFF! GLUB!
AWRIGHT, CAVALIER... I'LL GETCHA...
HALP!
YOW!
I CAN'T SWIM!
ME NEITHER!
AGAIN!
MOVE OVER, MINNIE! I'VE ALWAYS GOTTA RESCUE FOLKS!

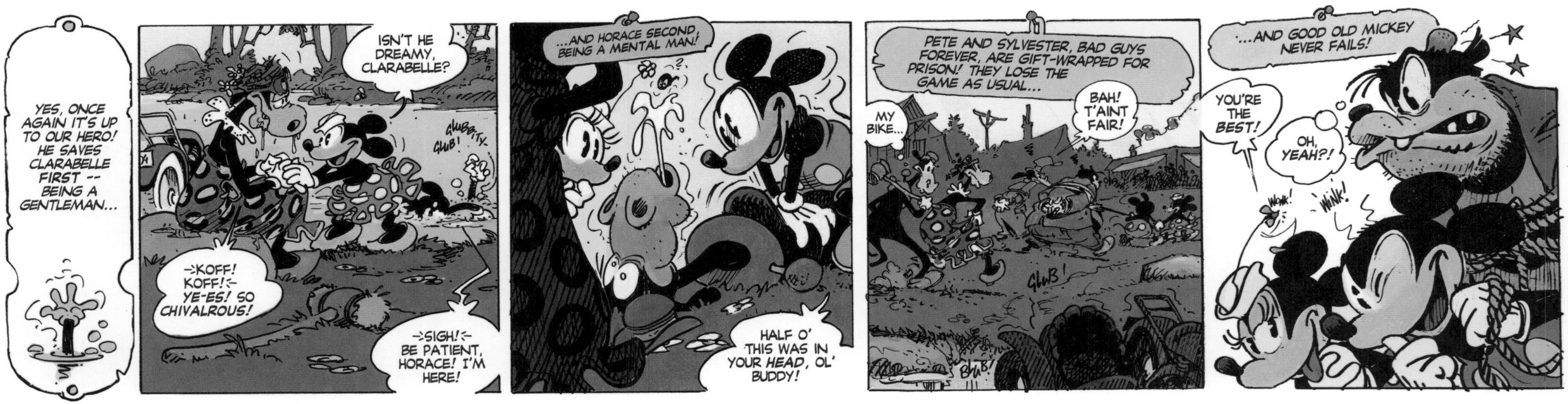
YES, ONCE AGAIN IT'S UP TO OUR HERO! HE SAVES CLARABELLE FIRST -- BEING A GENTLEMAN...
ISN'T HE DREAMY, CLARABELLE?
GLUBBITY GLUB!
KOFF! KOFF! YE-ES! SO CHIVALROUS!
SIGH! BE PATIENT, HORACE! I'M HERE!
...AND HORACE SECOND, BEING A MENTAL MAN!
HALF O' THIS WAS IN YOUR HEAD, OL' BUDDY!
PETE AND SYLVESTER, BAD GUYS FOREVER, ARE GIFT-WRAPPED FOR PRISON! THEY LOSE THE GAME AS USUAL...
MY BIKE...
BAH! T'AINT FAIR!
GLUB!
BLUB!
...AND GOOD OLD MICKEY NEVER FAILS!
YOU'RE THE BEST!
OH, YEAH?!
WONK!
WINK!

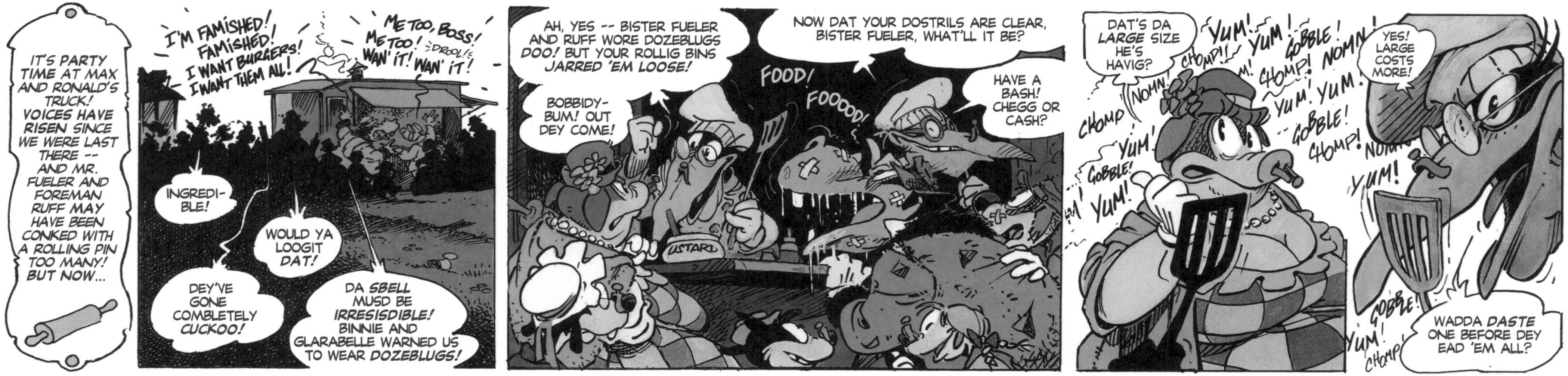
IT'S PARTY TIME AT MAX AND RONALD'S TRUCK! VOICES HAVE RISEN SINCE WE WERE LAST THERE -- AND MR. FUELER AND FOREMAN RUFF MAY HAVE BEEN CONKED WITH A ROLLING PIN TOO MANY! BUT NOW...
I'M FAMISHED! FAMISHED! I WANT BURGERS! I WANT THEM ALL!
ME TOO, BOSS! ME TOO! WAN' IT! WAN' IT!
DROOL!
INGREDI-BLE!
WOULD YA LOOGIT DAT!
DEY'VE GONE COMBLETELY CUCKOO!
DA SBELL MUSD BE IRRESISDIBLE! BINNIE AND GLARABELLE WARNED US TO WEAR DOZEBLUGS!
AH, YES -- BISTER FUELER AND RUFF WORE DOZEBLUGS DOO! BUT YOUR ROLLIG BINS JARRED 'EM LOOSE!
NOW DAT YOUR DOSTRILS ARE CLEAR, BISTER FUELER, WHAT'LL IT BE?
BOBBIDY-BUM! OUT DEY COME!
FOOD!
FOOOOD!
HAVE A BASH! CHEGG OR CASH?
DAT'S DA LARGE SIZE HE'S HAVIG?
YUM! YUM! GOBBLE! CHOMP! NOMN!
YES! LARGE COSTS MORE!
WADDA DASTE ONE BEFORE DEY EAD 'EM ALL?

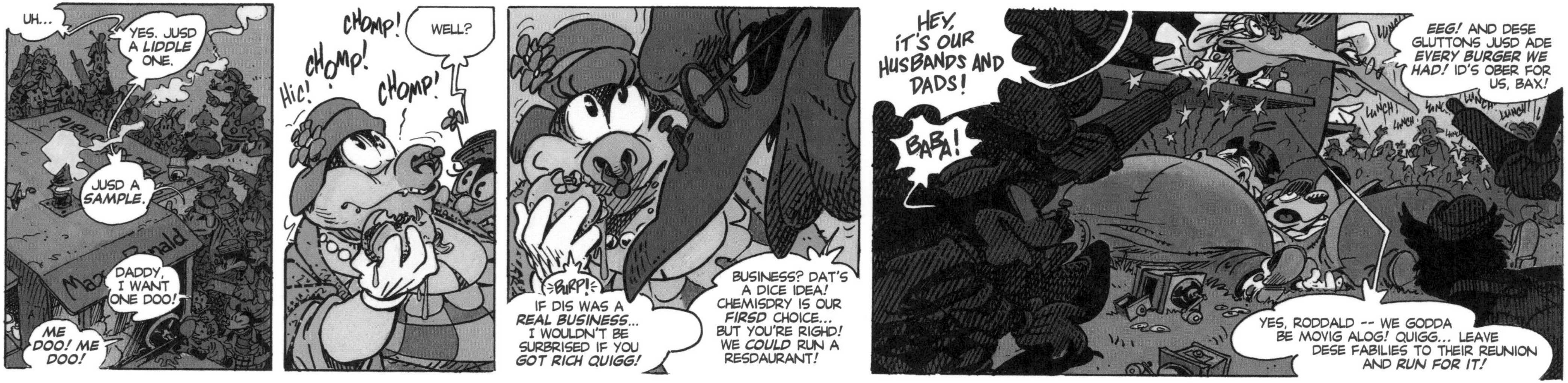
UH...
YES. JUSD A LIDDLE ONE.
JUSD A SAMPLE.
DADDY, I WANT ONE DOO!
ME DOO! ME DOO!
CHOMP! CHOMP! CHOMP! HIC!
WELL?
BURP!
IF DIS WAS A REAL BUSINESS... I WOULDN'T BE SURBRISED IF YOU GOT RICH QUIGG!
BUSINESS? DAT'S A DICE IDEA! CHEMISDRY IS OUR FIRSD CHOICE... BUT YOU'RE RIGHD! WE COULD RUN A RESDAURANT!
HEY, IT'S OUR HUSBANDS AND DADS!
BABA!
EEG! AND DESE GLUTTONS JUSD ADE EVERY BURGER WE HAD! ID'S OBER FOR US, BAX!
YES, RODDALD -- WE GODDA BE MOVIG ALOG! QUIGG... LEAVE DESE FABILIES TO THEIR REUNION AND RUN FOR IT!

SO... MOUSE-TON'S MOMS AND KIDS FIND THEIR DADS, THEIR DADS FIND THEIR LUNCHES... AND ALL'S WELL THAT ENDS WELL!
AH, YES! THERE'S STILL A DEPRES-SION ON! JOBS ARE STILL SPOTTY! BUT... NEVER AGAIN WILL FOLKS GRIND THE "ZOMBIE COFFEE" THAT TURNS THEM INTO ZOMBIES, ZERVANTS, AND ZTOOGES!
NO COFFEE FOR YOU! ONLY TEA FROM NOW ON!
YES, M'LOVE...
THINGS END A LITTLE LESS WELL FOR OUR VILLAINS IN THE CLINK -- BUT WE EXPECTED AS MUCH! THESE BAD BOYS HAVE ALREADY BEEN FORCED TO RESTORE EVERYTHING: REBUILD, REHOUSE, REFOREST, REIMBURSE, ETC. ETC.! MOUSETON'S UPPER WEST SIDE RECOVERS...
...AND ITS HOUSES RECOVER THEIR OWNERS! AS FAR AS MICKEY'S CONCERNED -- ONCE MORE, WITH FEELING: ALL'S WELL THAT ENDS DOGGONE WELL!
TO SUM UP, MAX: "FAST FOOD," BIG, FAT, CHEAP!
Z
DO YOU WANT FRIES WITH THAT?

- The End -

FRIES? ...I DUNNO!

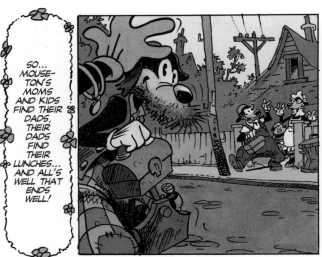

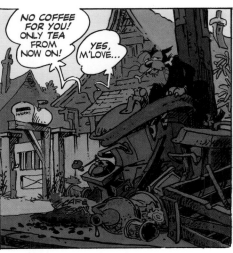

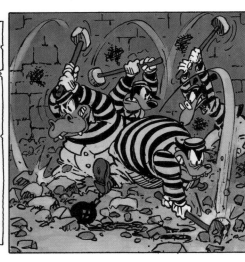

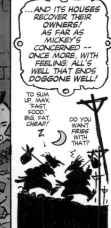

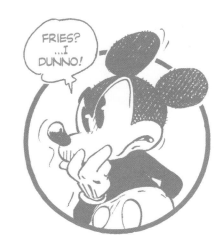

ALL THE PLAYERS IN THIS GREAT SOCIAL DRAMA

I'M TH' HERO, FOLKS!

YEAH, BUT I'M TH' DASHING DREAMBOAT!

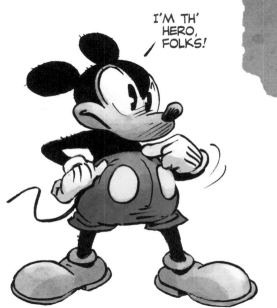

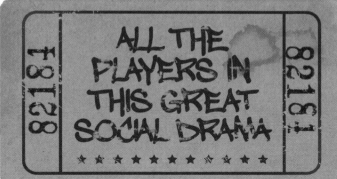

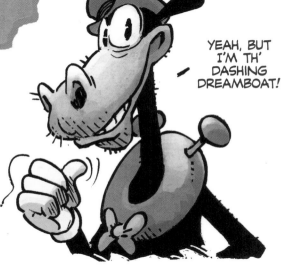

Mickey Mouse

as himself

Horace Horsecollar

as himself

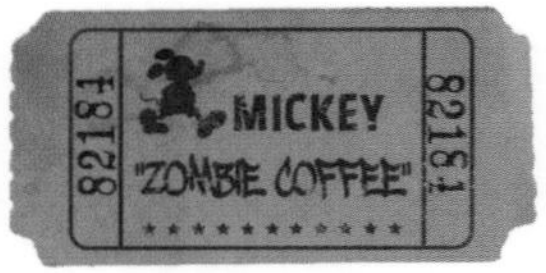
82181
MICKEY
"ZOMBIE COFFEE"
82181

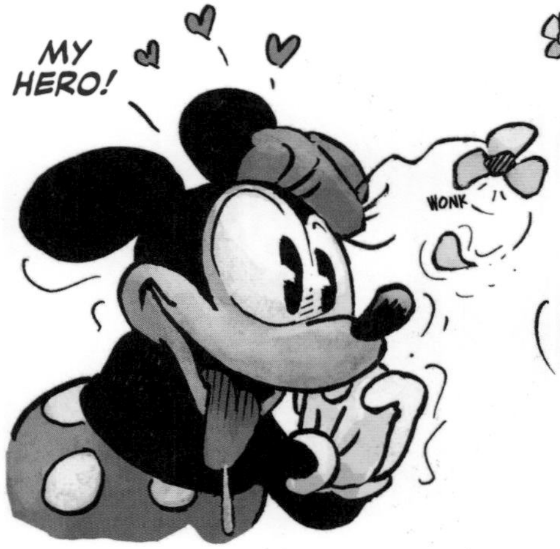
MY HERO!
WONK

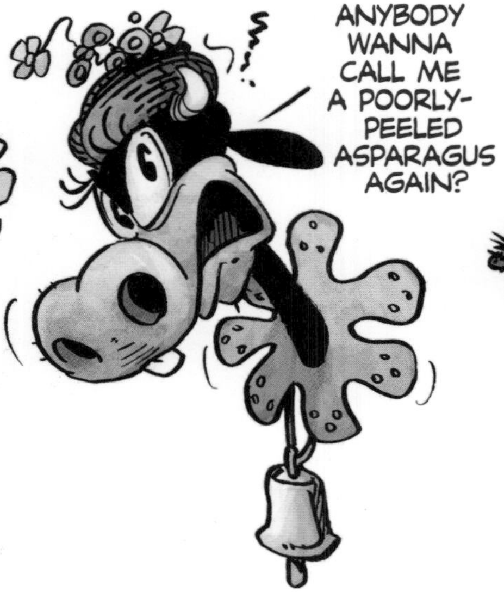
ANYBODY WANNA CALL ME A POORLY-PEELED ASPARAGUS AGAIN?

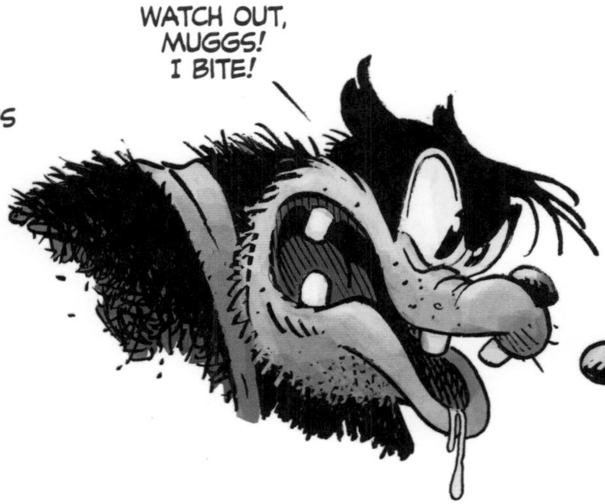
WATCH OUT, MUGGS! I BITE!

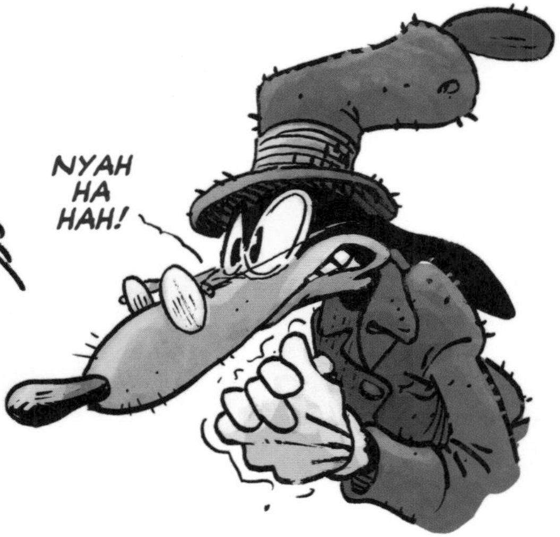
NYAH HA HAH!

Minnie Mouse

as herself

Clarabelle Cow

as herself

Peg-Leg Pete

as the bad guy

Sylvester

as a most remarkable, extraordinary fellow

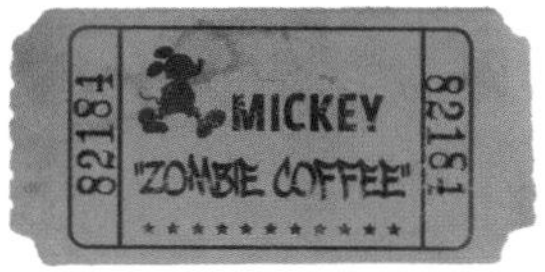
MICKEY
"ZOMBIE COFFEE"

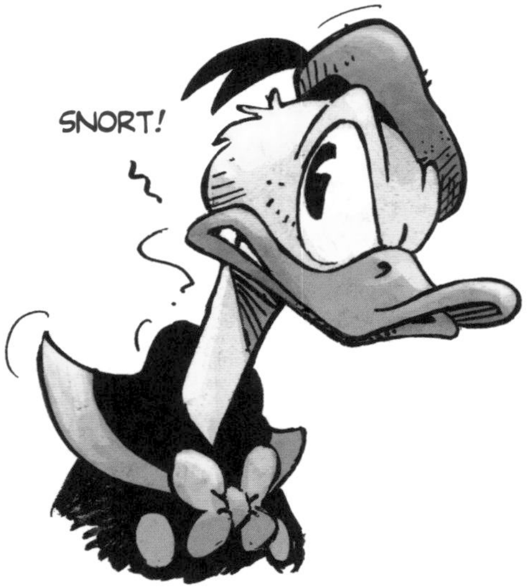
SNORT!

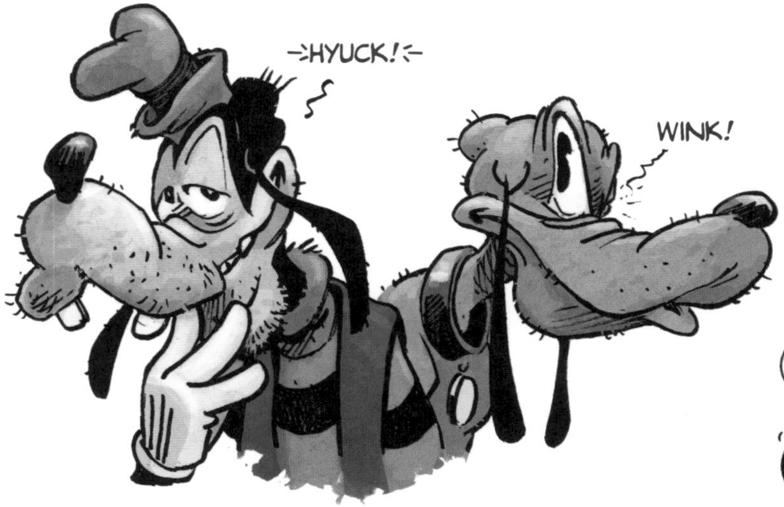
HYUCK!
WINK!

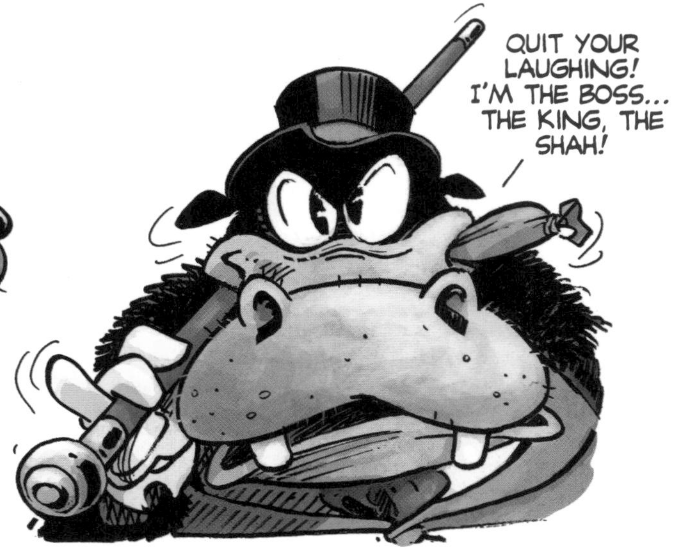
QUIT YOUR LAUGHING! I'M THE BOSS... THE KING, THE SHAH!

Donald Duck

as himself

Goofy

as himself

Pluto the Pup

as man's best friend (to wit) the dog

Rock Fueler

as the crooked banking tycoon

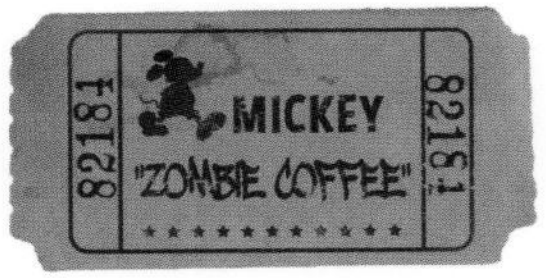
82181
MICKEY
"ZOMBIE COFFEE"
82181

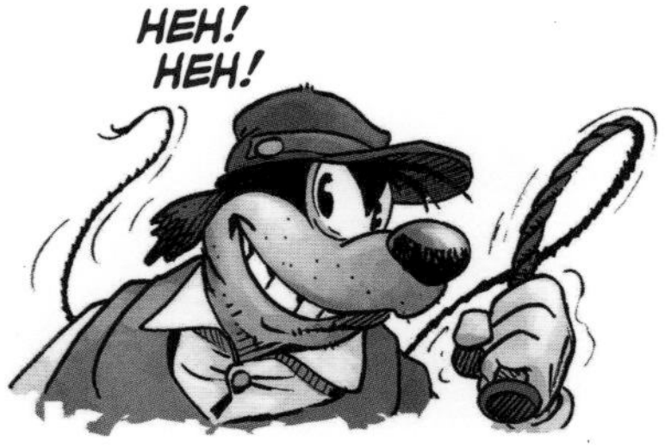
HEH! HEH!

Foreman Ruff

in a walk-on role

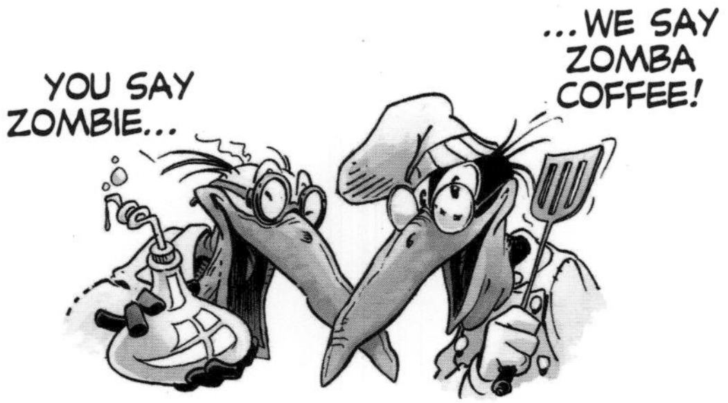
YOU SAY ZOMBIE...
...WE SAY ZOMBA COFFEE!

Max & Ronald

as the culinary chemists

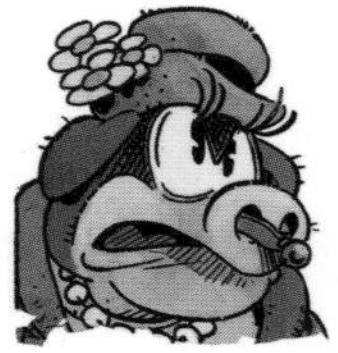

Elsa Porkski

as the rabble-rouser

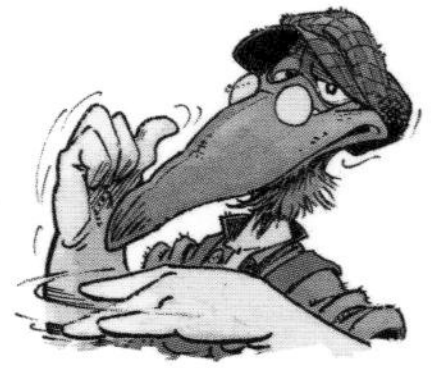

special thanks for the stellar contributions of

Bernie

CAUTION

The author wishes to reassure animal protection organizations and sensitive readers in regard to certain slapstick humor depicted. No cartoon animals were harmed in the making of this story.

Ms. Paula Pullet and Jojo the woodpecker are internationally renowned stuntbirds who, in spite of appearances, have not lost any of their feathers.

- Regis Loisel

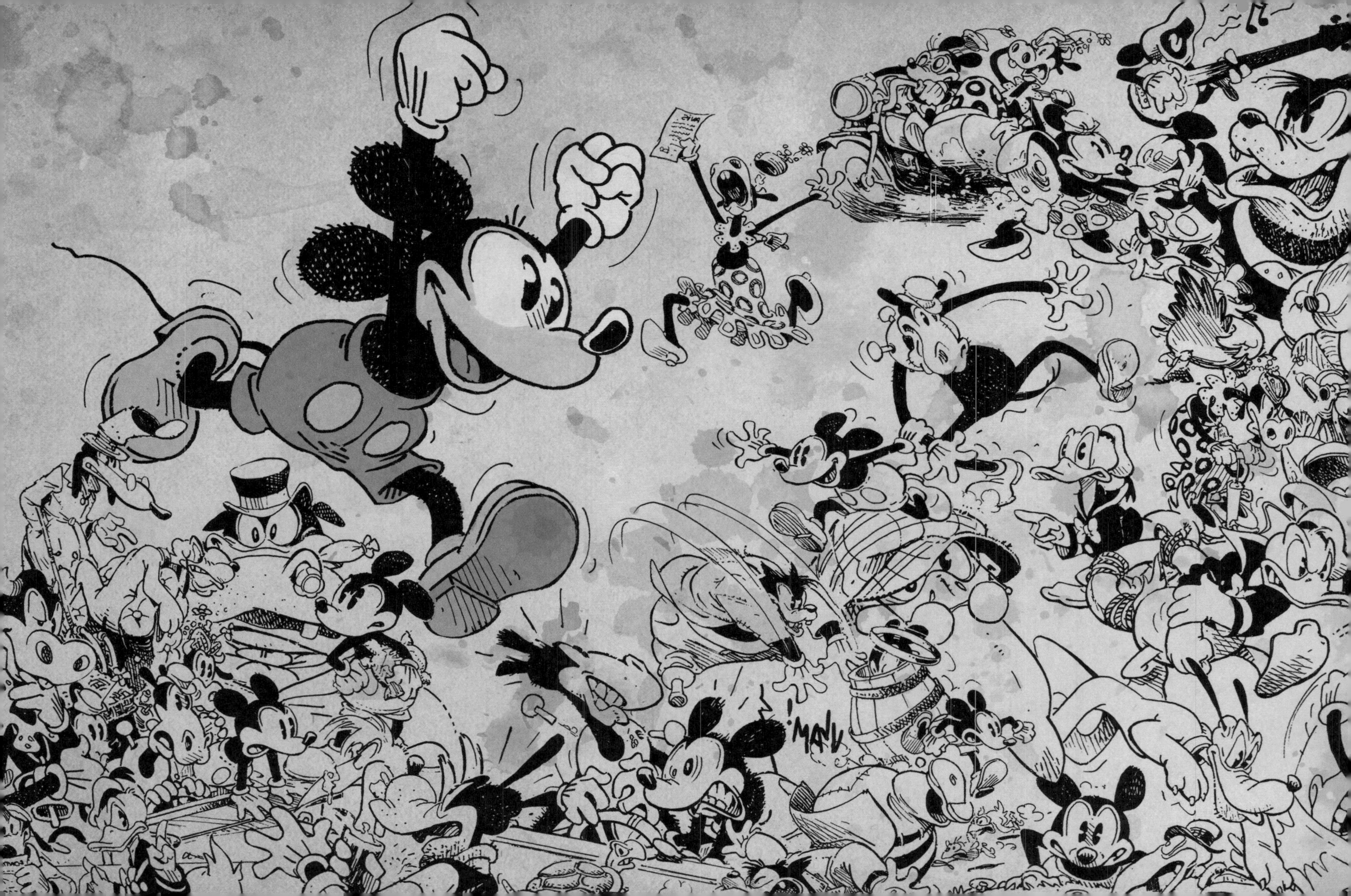
WHAM!